TOUCHED BY THE

FATHER'S

HAND

mark a. rivera
as told to
joanne jacquart

Stonecrest

Graphic situations are depicted. Names of some individuals
have been changed to protect their privacy.

Printed in the United States of America
First edition, first printing 1991

ISBN 0 9625097 2 8

Published by

Stonecrest Publications
117 Kerneywood Drive
Lakeland, Florida 33803

By arrangement with
Anchor House

DEDICATION

This book is gratefully dedicated to my Lord and Savior, Jesus Christ.

I also wish to dedicate this book to my wonderful family; Pam, Matthew and Theresa. It was through their support and love that I have been able to fulfill my calling at Anchor House.

Finally, it is dedicated to the many young men who have passed through Anchor House and who have been touched by our Lord through this ministry, especially in memory of Valentin Guttierrez. Valentin's relationship with our Lord was an example to all who knew him.

ACKNOWLEDGEMENTS

My appreciation and thanks to:

My writer, Joanne Jacquart, for the many hours of taping and the talent for taking my words and making them readable.

Maggie Bodé and the generous members of All Saints' Episcopal Church, Lakeland, Florida, whose financial assistance made this book possible.

Lou Britain, Rosemary Yates and Charles Weatherly for data entry.

Cindee Hansel, Ted Poitras, Jana Huss, Betty Jester, Syndi Briscoe and Rosemary and Davis Yates for proofing and editing.

Davis Yates for planning and layout.

Jeanie Solomon for the art rendering of this attractive cover.

I give thanks to the Holy Spirit for the guidance and burning determination inspired in the many people who were responsible for turning this manuscript into a book.

SPECIAL THANKS

With special thanks to my dear friends, editors and publishers—Davis and Rosemary Yates. I appreciate their persistence, determination and hard work in making this book a reality. They were moved to bring my dream to fruition and I am grateful.

Chapter One

"Hey, Rivera, we want to talk to you, man." It was a command, not a request.

Mark, Lefty and Bobby tensed and stopped in their tracks. They recognized the voice of a rival gang member, one of the Black Chaplains.

"Just be cool," Mark whispered to his two friends. "Remember the peace called at the board meeting."

One of the Chaplains swaggered over, crossed between them, and came up behind Mark.

"Hey, it's cool," Mark said. "Remember, there's a peace."

"The hell with the peace," he said, spitting on the ground.

"That's what the meeting was about," Mark said, standing his ground.

"Screw the Phantom Lords and the meetings," he shouted, glaring at each of them one by one.

Lefty stared back with a smirk on his face.

"What are you laughing about, jerk? Think this is funny, do you?" He pulled a switchblade out of his pocket and pressed the button. The blade snapped open with a soft click. Lefty froze.

"Hey, man, come on," Mark said. "What's your beef?"

"What's my beef?" He turned to Mark. "You're a stinkin' Spic. That's my beef." The other Black Chaplains snickered.

Lefty took off running down the narrow alley between the buildings and darted into the doorway leading to his house. "Run for it!" Bobby shouted to Mark. They bolted down the street in different directions. Bobby headed for the alley.

"Head for the park!" Mark yelled.

He hadn't gone far when he realized that the rest of the gang had moved in, blocking off the entire street. Mark came to a screeching halt, frantically glancing around for a doorway to disappear into. But it was too late.

A baseball bat slammed into Mark's gut. He let out a "whoooofff" of air grabbing his stomach.

"Look at the Puerto Rican pig now!" someone shouted, laughing.

The bat caught him against the side of his face. There was a crunching sound as wood struck bone. He fell to the ground. Someone kicked him.

"Let me stick him!"

"Yeah, kill the filthy Spic!"

Mark felt the searing pain of a steel blade in his side. His assailant plunged it in and out several times. On the third thrust, Mark passed out and the Chaplains left him for dead. Bobby had managed to get away in the confusion.

When Mark regained consciousness, he was lying in the street. The gutter was red with his blood. Moaning, he managed to half-walk, half-crawl, tripping and falling as he went. He made it to his house and stumbled through the door, blood splattering everywhere.

"Marco!" His mother screamed, "Oh my God, what happened?"

His body convulsed and dropped to the floor.

When he came to, he saw a Catholic priest leaning over him with Rosary beads, praying. Trying to fight through the haze in his mind, he suddenly realized he was in the hospital and some priest was giving him the last rites.

"Oh God," Mark cried. "Help me, please help me. Don't let me die." Haze engulfed him and he lost consciousness once again.

Over the next few days, Mark faded in and out of consciousness, muttering incoherently and then lapsing back into unreality. Sleep came in spurts of fretful dozing. His black hair was plastered to his forehead in wet ringlets. Fever ravaged his body.

Nightmarish memories and images trailed through his mind. San Juan, Puerto Rico. Age five. Stepping out of his house in the morning. Seeing his alcoholic father passed out in the front yard. Trying to pull and drag his heavy body up the front steps. His mother shouting. Crying. Being told that his father 'ran around with other women.' His mother telling him of the night his father stayed out partying. He was riding with some friends, sitting on the passenger side of the front seat. He sang at the top of his lungs, waving his arm out of the car window. In a drunken stupor, his buddy drove down the middle of the road. They passed an approaching car too close. Colliding, Mark's father lost his right arm in the accident.

His mother, pregnant with Mark at the time, visited his father in the hospital. Another pregnant woman showed up. More shouting and crying. Mark always wondered what his half-brother looked like. He had never even seen him.

Many times Mark's father, in a drunken stupor, shouted obscenities and threatened to kill everyone. His mother hustled Mark and Raphael, his full brother, off to a relative's house for a few days. When his father calmed down, they came back.

Lying in his hospital bed, now with a clear mind, Mark drifted back to his days in Puerto Rico. He remembered the day his mother announced that they were moving to New York.

"Things will be better there," she said. "We will have a new start."

"Will I go to school there?" Mark asked.

"Not right away," she said. "You and Raphael must stay in Puerto Rico."

"But I want to go with you," Mark cried.

"Your Aunt Josephine will take good care of you, Marco. You must help take care of your brother. Remember, you're the oldest."

Mark turned and ran to his room. His mother followed.

"We will send for you when we are settled. We have to find a place to live and find work."

Mark threw himself on the bed and covered his head with his pillow.

"Marco?"

He didn't answer.

His parents left when Mark was six years old. Although they kept in touch by letters, Mark felt abandoned. When letters arrived from his mother, Mark would sit and listen as Aunt Josephine read them out loud.

A whole year passed.

One day Aunt Josephine called him into the kitchen. Her voice sounded excited.

"They've sent for us," she said to Mark, waving the letter in her hand. "We're going to New York!"

"Really?"

"Yes. We're going on a ship called *The Marine Tiger*."

"I'll go get ready," Mark said, dashing off to his bedroom.

The ship arrived in New York Harbor on September 5, 1946, Mark's seventh birthday. Passengers crowded against the rails.

"Look! Over there!"

Adults lifted up their children so they could see.

Mark craned his neck and there it was—The Statue of Liberty. Bright and beautiful in the afternoon sun, she lifted her lamp in welcome.

"What a wonderful sight!" Aunt Josephine shouted.

Men and women jammed the rails, many weeping.

"We're home," a woman said. "We're finally home."

Tugboats pulled alongside the ship and passengers scrambled down rope ladders into the smaller boats. Mark squeezed into one of the boats with his younger brother.

His parents were waiting for them on the dock. His mother first greeted Aunt Josephine and then hugged the boys.

"I'm so glad to see you!" she said. "How I missed you!"

Mark's father politely reached out his left arm and shook hands with Mark and Raphael. He was sober.

They hurried through the bustle of people, noise and baggage.

"We are going to ride on the subway," his mother said.

"Subway?"

"Yes, this one is called 'The Elevator.' "

Before Mark had a chance to ask why it was called 'The Elevator,' he was whisked on board one of the cars. He pressed his face against the dirty glass of the window. The subway rattled and rumbled into the darkness.

"This isn't an elevator," Mark said to his mother. "It's a train." "It's called an elevator because we will be going from the underground tunnel, up and over the Williamsburg Bridge, crossing the East River."

Just then, they burst out of the tunnel.

"Look at all the lights!" Mark shouted.

Outside, the bright lights and multicolored signs blinked on and off in the early evening dusk. The subway lurched to a stop.

"Is this where we get off?"

"No, Marco. This is Marcy Avenue. Two stops, then we get off."

At Flushing Avenue, they scrambled out with all their luggage and walked down a long flight of cement steps.

Mark looked up at the towering buildings of the New York skyline. Clothes lines hung from fire escapes. The busy sidewalks were full of people selling newspapers and fruit from little stands. Music blared out into the street from at least a dozen radios.

"Where are we?" Mark asked, placing his hands over his ears.

"Brooklyn," his mother said.

Chapter Two

Mark and his family lived in a first floor apartment in an Italian neighborhood in Brooklyn. The first morning Mark woke up to the sound of voices in the street.

"Ice-a-man, Ice-a-man."

"Fish—fresh-a-fish."

Mark scrambled out of bed and ran to the front window. The ice man unloaded a big chunk of ice from his horse-drawn cart and hoisted it onto his shoulder, grasping it with a large pair of tongs. An elderly Italian lady, wearing a dark dress and an apron, scurried in front of him, waving her arms, pointing the way to her apartment. The ice would be placed in her icebox. For a quarter her food would stay fresh.

Other carts contained fresh fish; some carried fruit and vegetables. The street became a marketplace. Mark watched through the window as one peddler struggled to start his truck by turning the crank in front.

"Want to go outside?"

Startled by his father's voice, Mark jumped.

"You can go out if you want to."

Mark hesitated. Everything was new and strange to him. Life in Puerto Rico was certainly not like this.

"Go ahead. It's safe," his father chuckled. "The Italians are real nice people. Might as well enjoy them while you can. They're gradually moving out."

"Why?"

8

"Because too many 'low-class' Puerto Ricans are moving into the area. That's why." Annoyance came through in his voice. "The Italians aren't going to put up with them. You might as well get to know the streets around here. Just a few blocks down, if you turn right, you'll run into the blacks. If you turn left, the Polish."

Mark didn't understand why his father called other Puerto Ricans 'low-class'. What was the difference? He never dared ask his father too many questions. It could bring on one of his angry outbursts. Especially if he had been drinking, like this morning. He could smell the wine on his breath. Mark got dressed and went outside to explore his new neighborhood.

Mark's mother worked as a seamstress in a sewing factory. She also sewed at home, making most of their clothes. His father taught trumpet and gave guitar lessons. Coming to America, however, hadn't helped his drinking problem. Every night his mother and father fought about something.

When Mark was nine years old, he and his brother were sitting in the living room watching the murder mystery, "Danger", on television. His mother was in the kitchen, doing dishes and cleaning up the old cast iron stove after supper. His father sat at a small desk in the corner, writing a letter. There was a knock at the door. "Answer the door," his father shouted at Mark. Mark scrambled to the door and swung it open. Two women with grim faces glared down at Mark.

"Who is it?" his father asked.

The younger of the two women stepped inside. She was obviously pregnant. Mark's father looked surprised. His face paled.

"It's him," the young woman said. "That's my husband!"

"You do this to my niece and then just leave her?" The older woman screamed. "What kind of a man are you?"

"I don't know what you're talking about," Mark's father shouted back at her. "Get out of my house."

"You're a stinking liar. This is your child I'm carrying." The young woman burst into tears.

Mark ran into the kitchen. "Mommy! Come quick! There's a lady at the door and she said Daddy's her husband!"

His mother's face darkened. She brushed past Mark and marched into the living room. "What is this all about?" she asked. Her voice trembled.

The older woman said, "That man is my niece's husband. We've been tracking him down."

"You're crazy!" Mark's father shouted. "I don't even know who you are. Get out of my house!" He began trying to push them out the door.

"You're a liar!" the young woman screamed, striking out at him with her fists. "You're my husband and the father of my child!" Angry tears streamed down her face.

Mark's father shoved them outside and slammed the door shut.

His mother stood there, motionless. The sounds of screaming and sobbing filtered through the door. Her face flushed with anger.

"That's it! That's all I can take, Roberto." Her voice remained under control, but you could hear the contempt in it. "I've had nine years of this stuff." She gave a choked, desperate cry. "No more!" She spun around and stomped into the bedroom, slamming the door behind her.

Mark and his brother huddled in front of the television, afraid to say anything. When their father poured himself another glass of wine, cursed under his breath and sullenly plopped into a living room chair, they slipped off to their own bedroom. All through the night Mark heard the sounds of his mother's sobbing.

The next day Mark came home from school to eat lunch, as he usually did almost daily. His mother would take a sandwich to work and eat right at the factory. Sometimes Mark stopped by to see her on his way back to school. He stepped into the apartment and walked down the hallway to the bathroom. Then he heard noises and a commotion coming from the kitchen.

He walked slowly down the hall and peered into the kitchen. His father towered over his mother, threatening her with a knife.

"No! Stop it!" Mark screamed, dashing into the room. He jumped on his father's back, grabbing him around the neck. Desperately, he struggled to pull his father away from his mother. They twisted and turned, his father trying to shake Mark off his back. The knife lashed out into the air, coming dangerously close to his mother. They stumbled and fell to the floor and his father dropped the knife. Mark lunged for it.

"Don't you hurt my mother!" he shouted, pointing the knife toward his father. Fear and anger knotted inside of him.

"Shut up!" his father yelled, scrambling back to his feet, snatching the knife from Mark.

Mark ran to the other side of the kitchen and picked up a hammer lying on the counter. He lifted it over his head to throw it.

"No, Marco...No!" his mother screamed. "Don't hit your father!"

The color suddenly drained from his father's face and he collapsed on the floor, sobbing. His mother stumbled across the room.

"That's it," she cried. "I want you out of this house today." Her voice broke and her body began to shake with sobs. She dashed towards the bathroom, almost knocking Mark over as she ran past him.

His father sat on the kitchen floor, slumped against the cupboards. He covered his face with his hands and wept aloud, rocking back and forth.

Trembling, Mark placed the hammer back on the counter and ran out the front door. He wondered why his mother had yelled at him to stop. He was only trying to protect her. Why did she take his father's side?

Mark didn't stop running until he reached the Catholic church. Out of breath, he hid under one of the pews, his heart pounding and his body shaking. He listened. It was quiet. Slipping out from beneath the pew, he stood in front of the statue of Christ's Crucifixion. Mary was holding Jesus in her arms after He was taken down from the cross. He stared at it for a long time. A single tear rolled down his cheek.

"Why did they do that to you, Jesus? You were only trying to help." More tears slowly found their way down his cheeks.

"What are you doing, Little Flower?"

Startled, Mark jumped, quickly wiping away the tears with his shirt sleeve. It was Father Fiore. He had called Mark "Little Flower" ever since the day Mark had asked him what "Fiore" meant.

"Fiore? It means 'flower.' How about if I call you 'Little Flower?' " he had laughed.

Mark grinned sheepishly. The name stuck.

"Why are you so sad today?" Father Fiore asked. "Are those tears I see?" He brushed a remaining tear from Mark's face.

Mark took a deep breath. "I want to be a priest," Mark said.

"Well, you certainly are one of my best altar boys," he said, "You already know the entire mass and you are faithful to come here every day to help with whatever needs to be done. But making a decision to become a priest is pretty serious business. What brought this on?"

Mark shrugged, then asked, "If I become a priest, can I live here?"

"Ahh...problems at home again." He put his arm around Mark's shoulder. "Life is hard sometimes, isn't it, Little Flower?"

Mark nodded.

"Do you want to talk about it?"

Mark shook his head no.

Father Fiore sighed. "Well, at least I'm glad you know where to come when things get rough." He looked down affectionately at Mark. "Come with me," he said. "Let's sit and talk about faraway places. Have I ever told you about the Riviera?"

"No," Mark said.

Father Fiore's eyes sparkled as he began to describe one of his trips to the Riviera and for a little while Mark was caught up in the excitement of traveling to beautiful places, forgetting about the problems at home.

When Mark walked into the house later that afternoon, his Aunt Josephine and his mother stood solemnly in the living room. A suitcase sat on the floor next to his father.

"Here's your ticket back to Puerto Rico, Roberto." Aunt Josephine said. "Leave, and don't ever come back here. We want nothing to do with you."

His mother stared straight ahead and said nothing. Mark stood by her side.

His father took the airline ticket, picked up his suitcase and started out the door. Then he turned, as if to say something, but changed his mind. He left without speaking.

Mark wondered if he would ever see him again.

Chapter Three

"Raphael, where are you?" Mark called, plunking his school books down on the kitchen table. There was no answer.

When Mark's father left, Mark had to drop out of sports at school in order to take care of his younger brother. At times he resented it, but he knew his mother worked hard at the sewing factory just to pay the bills and keep food on the table. Babysitting was Mark's way of helping out.

"Raphael?" He walked through the house, but his younger brother wasn't there.

Mark went back outside and glanced up the street. A block away he noticed a scuffle going on with a small neighborhood gang. This had become a regular occurrence on their street. Mark walked toward the boys to see what it was about. That's when he heard his brother's voice.

"Marco, help me!"

Mark charged into the group of boys several years younger than himself. Raphael was kicking everyone in sight, cursing, screaming, and striking out with his hands and feet. And each member of the gang was fighting back.

"Stop it!" Mark shouted, pulling one boy at a time off of his brother. "Leave him alone!"

Raphael got even more brave with Mark in the middle of the fight and began cursing and screaming at them even louder. Mark felt the sting of a bicycle chain across his arm. Another boy slashed him with a broken bottle and Mark felt the warm blood ooze out of a gash in his leg. Although he was stronger than any of them, Mark was out-numbered.

"Raphael, get the hell out of here," he yelled at his brother.

Raphael ignored him and continued to attack, arms and fists swinging. Mark finally managed to fight off the boys and grabbed Raphael by his shirt, pulling him, kicking and screaming back to the house.

"Are you crazy?" He shouted at Raphael when they stepped inside. "Why can't you learn to keep your mouth shut and stay out of trouble? You're always starting fights. That wise mouth of yours will get you killed some day."

The door swung open.

"What's all the shouting about?" Their mother stood in the doorway. She looked at Raphael, clothes torn and dirty, then at Mark, bruised and bleeding.

"Marco! What happened? Can't I even depend on you to watch your little brother? I work hard all day and this is what I come home to!"

She walked over to Raphael and put her arms around him. "Raphael, my poor baby, are you okay?"

Raphael glanced over at Mark and smirked, trying to maintain a wide-eyed look of innocence.

She turned on Mark and said, "Are you running with one of those gangs on the streets? Is that what this is all about?"

"No...I just..."

"You better not be. All they do is fight and cause trouble in the neighborhood. You're supposed to protect your little brother from all that. You're the oldest. You should set a good example for your brother to follow."

Mark stood silently before her, head bowed. It would do no good to try to explain.

"Go change your clothes, both of you."

Mark went into the bathroom and washed the blood off the gash in his leg. He changed his clothes, left the house, and walked down to the church. He worked there almost every day after his mother got home from work. He helped with the preparations for Mass and did whatever other little odd jobs needed to be done around the building. And he always looked forward to talking with Father Fiore.

He walked down to the basement where the cleaning supplies and the wine vats were kept. Noticing a dripping spout on one of the vats, he held his finger under it, then tasted the wine.

"Young man, what do you think you're doing?" The stern male voice startled Mark.

"I'm...I'm just here to clean up and help with preparations for the Mass," Mark answered.

"No, you're not. You're lying. You're sneaking around. I saw you drinking the wine." He grabbed Mark by the arm and his fingers dug into Mark's flesh. "Don't you know that's a sin?" His voice grated harshly.

"I didn't mean anything," Mark said. "I'm sorry, Father." This was a new priest Mark hadn't seen before.

Two nuns heard the commotion and scurried over to them. The priest told the nuns that he had caught Mark drinking from the wine vats.

"It's a sin to be drinking the wine," one of them said with a tone of disgust. "You will be suspended for this."

"Where is Father Fiore?" Mark asked, jerking his arm free from the priest's grasp.

"He left for Rome," Father Monterey answered.

"When will he be back?"

"Here? Probably never. He's been given a new assignment."

"He's gone?" Mark couldn't believe it. The priest hadn't even bothered to say good-bye.

"That's right. Now, about your suspension of duties."

Mark turned and dashed out of the church before Father Monterey completed the sentence.

Why hadn't Father Fiore called to tell him he had to leave? He thought they were friends. Friends don't leave without saying good-bye.

He wandered aimlessly down the street. With Father Fiore gone, he had no place to run. He stopped and sat down on a street corner. He thought about the movie he saw at the church recently. It was about a little boy named Marcelino who lived in a monastery with the priests. In the story, Marcelino took bread from the priest's table every day and disappeared with it. When questioned by the priests about what he was doing with the bread, Marcelino wouldn't answer. One day one of the priests secretly followed the little boy. Marcelino went into the storage room and sat on a chair pulled up in front of a crucifix.

"I brought you some food," Marcelino said to Jesus on the cross. "I know you must be hungry. You've been up there a long time." The priest listened at the door.

Marcelino placed the bread in front of the cross and left the storage room. When the priest checked back later, the bread was gone. This continued on for several days, with the priest listening at the door. One day the priest heard another voice coming from inside. It said, "Marcelino, if I gave you a wish, what would you want?"

"To be with my mother," the little boy said. "I really miss her since she died." The priest waited and listened. There was silence. He slowly opened the door to peek in. Marcelino sat on the chair as if some invisible person was holding him. The priest called his name, but Marcelino didn't answer.

"I wish I were dead," Mark whispered to himself, wiping his eyes.

"Hey, Mark!" It was Boonzi running down the sidewalk towards Mark. "What are you doing?"

"Nothin'. What does it look like I'm doing?"

"We need one more for our stickball game. Want to play?"

Mark sighed.

"Come on."

"Okay."

After the game, Boonzi said, "Cook Street is planning some action tonight. Want to get in on it?"

"Yeah," Mark said. "Why not."

"All right!" Boonzi said, slapping Mark on the back. "It's about time you joined us. You've been missing out on all the fun. Come on, I'll help you put together a carpet gun."

They created a weapon out of a sawed-off broom handle, clothes pin, rubber bands, and pieces of carpet. When hit with it, the victim would get small cuts and welts.

When the street gangs came together that night, Mark fought with a vengeance. He did more than his share of damage and the others in the gang loved it. Running with the Cook Street gang became a daily thing. Mark felt accepted and got a high from rumbling with rival street gangs. Fighting became a way of life. But it didn't stop there.

One day Mark was walking across the school yard heading home, when he heard music. Looking around, he saw a group of older guys hanging out in a corner of the yard. Two played bongo drums and several others sang in harmony. Mark wandered over to listen.

"Hey kid, you like our music?"

"Yeah, it's pretty good."

"Pretty good, huh? And here we were thinkin' we were great." They all laughed.

"Come on, kid, you're okay." The two playing the bongos put them down. "Want a reefer?"

Mark hesitated.

"Come on, man. You mean you've never tried it?"

Mark shook his head no.

"It'll make you feel good."

One of the guys lit one up and handed it to Mark. He took it and began to puff. It had a strange, sweet taste.

"Hey, kid, this is how you do it."

Mark watched.

"Take a long drag and hold it in."

Mark inhaled and immediately felt the dizzying effects of the weed.

"Wow," he said. "It's like being in a slow-motion movie."

"Now you got it," they laughed. "Feels pretty good, huh?"

Mark nodded yes.

"Well, just remember that we've got the best stuff around. There's always more where that came from."

Mark walked home from school feeling better than he had felt in a long time. Smoking pot and drinking became part of his daily routine as he worked his way up within the gangs.

Chapter Four

Mark remained in school, but spent more and more of his time on the streets running with the gangs. He graduated from the Cook Street gang to the Phantom Lords. This meant giving up baseball bats, bicycle chains and carpet guns for brass knuckles, sawed-off shotguns and switchblades. He came close to death several times, especially that one time when he ended up in a coma in the hospital and the priest stood over him giving him the last rites of the church.

He liked the excitement of the street fights and the acceptance he felt from the gang members. But every now and then he felt a twinge of guilt when he thought about the struggle his mother was going through. She worked hard and Mark knew she worried about him.

One night while he walked home, he decided to try to build a better relationship with her, even though she made him angry for taking Raphael's side most of the time. After all, Raphael was her "baby." If she only knew that he instigated more trouble than Mark did! Most of Mark's fighting took place within the realm of gang warfare. Raphael walked around with a chip on his shoulder and a sarcastic attitude. But he sure knew how to manipulate his mother.

Mark sighed as he walked in the front door. He'd just try a little harder to make things better at home. Like tonight, coming home earlier than usual and just spending some time with his mother.

Hearing muffled voices coming from down the hall, he headed for his mother's bedroom. Laughter filtered through the door. He hadn't heard his mother laugh in a long time. But something didn't feel right. When he tapped on the door the room grew quiet.

"Mom? It's me."

Not getting an answer, he swung the door open.

"What are you doing home?" His mother's voice was cold and lashing. She jerked the sheets up over her naked body. The man laying next to her bolted up and sat on the edge of the bed. He said nothing.

"What's going on here?" Mark's face twisted in shock, then clouded into anger.

"It's none of your business. Now get out!"

Mark stood in the doorway, fists clenched at his sides. "You called my father a 'womanizer'," his voice dropped in volume, but revealed the white-hot anger rising within, "Well, maybe he was. But you're a whore!"

She jumped out of bed with the sheet wrapped around her nude body and slapped him hard across the face.

"Don't you dare speak to me like that!"

Hurt and hatred blazed in Mark's eyes. He spun around and stormed out of the house.

Outside, he felt anger rising, sharp and bitter, in his throat. He swallowed once, twice, three times before the tightness in his throat would ease. Tears were the ultimate sign of weakness. With bitter anger knotting his stomach, he marched down the sidewalk.

"Hey, Mark, what's buggin' you?" It was his new friend, Apache, a member of the Dragons.

"What do you mean, what's buggin' me?" Mark snapped.

"Your face, man. It's written all over your face."

"Nothin's buggin' me," Mark said in a cold, steel voice.

"Okay, man. Okay." Apache said. "Listen, I talked to Pale Face Ralphy about you."

"So?"

"He said that since you've been a good member of the Phantom Lords in Brooklyn, he'd let you join the Dragons over in East Harlem. He heard you were a good fighter."

"What makes you think I want to join the Dragons?"

"Hey, everybody wants to move up through the ranks. This is a move up for you. You don't even have to go through the normal initiation. What do you say?"

Mark looked at Apache standing there in his bell bottoms, sporting the black and green Dragon jacket, wearing a narrow-brimmed hat and carrying a cane. He broke into a smile.

"Don't you know you could get picked up by the cops for wearing that jacket on the street? You lookin' for trouble? They dragged a couple of guys down the station the other night for wearing their membership jacket."

"Hey, I'm proud to be a Dragon. We're the best." He tapped his cane on the pavement to make his point. "And you need to join up with us. Then you can have some of these fine threads too." He paraded in a circle around Mark.

"Okay," Mark laughed. "You win."

"Now you're talkin'," Apache said. "And just in time for the fun. Tonight we're going to teach the Enchanters a lesson. When we're through, they'll know they went up against the Dragons."

"Let's go get 'em," Mark said.

They joined the other Dragons at their clubhouse and gathered their weapons. Zip guns, sawed-off shotguns, clubs, knives, bayonets. Anything that could cause destruction.

Then they swarmed into the Enchanters' neighborhood, shooting out windows, smashing headlights of cars, throwing broken bottles and bricks. Everyone was laughing and shouting, enjoying the violence that had become a normal part of their lives. Someone opened a car door and slashed the seats. Several others jumped up and down on the hood and roof, smashing it with clubs.

Mark heard gunshots, but couldn't tell where they came from. Sirens wailed in the distance.

"Let's blow, here come the cops!"

The gang scattered in all directions.

Later, one by one, they all drifted into the soda shop near their clubhouse. They handed the weapons to their girls and the girls hid the guns under their clothing. New York City law prohibited a policeman from searching a female.

One of the girls slipped down from the soda fountain and turned on the juke box. It blared out 50's music.

Mark stood in the middle of the room and started singing along, "Some people say a man is made out of mud..."

Everyone started laughing and hooting.

"Sing it, Mark!"

Suddenly a squad car screeched to a stop in front of the building, red lights blinking.

"Just stay cool," Mark said.

Two policemen burst through the front doors.

"Okay, you punks, we know what you did tonight."

"Why, officer," one of the girls purred, "these gentlemen have been with us all evening."

The gang snickered.

"Up against the counter," one of the cops shouted at Mark and Apache.

They frisked them, but found nothing.

"I told you officer—sir," one of the girls said.

Angry, the policemen turned to leave.

"Stop by anytime," she said, swaggering alongside them to the door.

The thudding sound of a gun hitting the floor brought instant silence to the room. It had slipped out from under the girl's dress.

Smirking, the police officer slowly bent over and picked it up.

"Well, well. What do we have here?"

The girl backed against a wall. The fear on her face wasn't because of the cops. She was afraid of what the Dragons would do to her for being so stupid.

"Okay, everybody's coming down to the station." He turned and told his partner to call for backup.

At the station house, those picked up were separated into different rooms and questioned individually.

Mark refused to talk.

"We know right where you were tonight," one of the detectives said. "One of your friends already told us all about it."

"You're lying," Mark spat out. "And I don't know nothin'."

"Two kids in the hospital and you don't know anything about it."

"That's right."

"Two 'Enchanters' in the hospital." He glared at Mark.

"Who cares about those scum?" Mark stared back at him.

"You know what? You're nothing but a piece of garbage." He got up out of his seat and headed towards Mark. "Get up."

Mark stood to his feet, trying not to show the fear that he felt.

"Move." He shoved Mark towards the door.

Mark walked ahead of the officer down the corridor. Another officer joined them and they stepped outside of the building, into an alley.

"What do you see?" the detective asked Mark.

Mark looked around.

"Garbage cans," he said.

"Right. And you're a piece of garbage." He grabbed Mark and stuffed him into one of the cans.

The two officers howled.

"How does it feel?"

"He should feel right at home."

After they had their fun with him, mocking him and slapping him around, the officers brought him back inside and booked him. Mark and several other gang members were sent to the state reformatory school in Warwick for one year.

His first night out, Mark went to a "welcome home" party with his old gang members. Someone handed him a capsule.

"Try this. It'll really turn you on."

Mark held it in his hand. "How much do these cost?" he asked.

"Fifty cents."

"Not bad." He broke open the capsule and snorted it. The next thing he knew he was vomiting all over the place.

"Forget that stuff," Mark groaned, holding his stomach.

They all howled in laughter.

"You've been away too long. You need to mainline it, man. You'll feel out of this world."

The next night that's exactly what he did. He felt an immediate rush and experienced a new high.

"This is great stuff," he said. He was hooked on heroin.

In order to pay for his supply of drugs, Mark became a courier for a connection between Brooklyn and East Harlem. He never had to worry about having enough smack for his own personal stash.

Chapter Five

Mark glanced in the bathroom mirror.

"You'll sweep her off her feet," he said to himself. "How could she possibly resist such a face, such charm?"

He grabbed his cane, clicked his wing-tip shoes, and headed out the door.

He had a date with Annette, who lived in Viceroy territory. The Dragons and Viceroys had called a peace, so Mark didn't expect any trouble.

Humming a tune as he swaggered up to her apartment, he tapped on the door with his cane.

Annette swung open the door. She wore a black skirt and a red sweater. Both hugged her figure. Her long, jet-black hair was tied back into a ponytail, tied with a red scarf.

Mark let out a wolf whistle. "Hey, Baby, you look great," he said.

"Thanks." She smiled and her eyes sparkled.

As they walked down the sidewalk, Mark slipped his arm around her waist. She snuggled her body close to his.

Suddenly, Mark heard running footsteps behind him. Before he had a chance to turn around, he felt the gun in his back.

"Move, Spic. Into that hallway." The voice spoke with terse, clipped words through clenched teeth.

Mark glanced over his shoulder. It was Benny, a member of the Viceroys. He had three others with him.

"We're taking you up to the roof and throwing you off, Spic."

"Yeah," another said, "And we'll watch your greasy, stinkin' body splatter all over the sidewalk."

Annette began screaming.

"Help! Somebody help! Please!" Her eyes were wild with fear.

They shoved her aside and she darted down the street, screaming, "Help! Please! Somebody!"

They pushed Mark into a dark, dingy hallway. The stench of urine, smoke, and grease made him gag. Someone whacked him across the back with a lead pipe. He fell to the floor.

"What's the matter, Spic, don't know how to walk?"

Mark started to get up.

"Well, maybe your cane would help." Mark felt a sharp pain as the cane whacked him in the back of his head.

Benny and the rest of the Viceroys roared with laughter as Mark fell to the floor again. He knew they meant business. This wasn't a game. Several other gang members had been found dead before this last peace was called.

Mark struggled to his feet. "But we called a peace," he said.

"Well, we called a Jap," Benny said. "Don't you remember Pearl Harbor?"

"You expect a stupid Spic to know about Pearl Harbor?" another jeered.

"After we drop him off the roof on his head, he won't know nothin', that's for sure!"

"Yeah, he'll be history!"

They all laughed.

Fear. Stark, terrifying fear filled Mark.

"God, help me," he cried out within himself.

"Enough talk!" They slammed Mark against the wall.

"Move!" they shouted, forcing him up the steps to the rooftop. They kicked him repeatedly as he stumbled up the stairs.

Reaching the top, Benny pushed open the door to the tarred rooftop.

They all froze. A cop stood in the doorway.

"Damn!" Benny cursed.

Everyone turned, Mark included, and scrambled down the stairs. Tripping and falling over each other, they scattered in different directions when they hit the street. Mark hid back in the shadows of one of the alleys until he was sure things were clear.

"What a lucky break," he said to himself. "That cop must have been checking the roof for junkies."

He darted in and out of alleys, working his way back home. His heart pounded so hard, he was afraid someone might hear him.

The next morning he got up aching all over. His eyes were running and he couldn't stop yawning. He needed a fix. After he copped some smack he felt much better.

Now it was 'get even' time. Rounding up a few of the Dragons, including Apache, Mark headed for enemy territory. They snagged the first rival member they came across, bringing him back to their turf.

"You think you can just grab one of our members and get away with it?" Apache sneered.

They dragged him down a side street and into a basement entrance under a flight of stairs in an apartment building. Papers and trash were everywhere. The stairwell stank of stale urine.

"A little Apache torture should make us even," Mark said in a cold steel voice.

The boy's eyes grew wide with horror. He began kicking, cursing and screaming. But he was outnumbered.

Mark ripped off the boy's shirt. It took all of them to wrestle him to the ground and tie him down.

"Hey, let's give him something to remember us by." Apache said.

They continued the slow torture until the boy passed out. Then they dumped his body back in his own territory as a lesson to the other Viceroys.

"Tell your friends they'd better not mess with us," Apache said. "Or they'll all get what you got. Maybe worse!"

The boy lay crumpled on the ground. He didn't respond.

Chapter Six

"Where have you been?" Mark's mother demanded. She looked into his eyes and knew he was high again.

"Out," Mark said.

"What kind of answer is that? Out. Where, out? What have you been doing?"

"Nothing."

"Nothing. You've been out. Doing nothing."

"I was just with my friends," Mark said. He walked over to the kitchen sink to wash his hands before getting something to eat.

His mother marched right behind him and pulled up his shirt sleeves.

"What is that on your arms?"

"What are you talking about?" Mark jerked his sleeves back down.

"What am I talking about?" Her voice rose. "Those marks on your arm." She yanked his shirt sleeve up again and pointed. "Those dots."

Mark didn't answer.

"I'm not going to support a junkie," she screamed. "First your father with his drinking, now you with your drugs!" She burst into tears.

"Shut up!" Mark shouted. "Just leave me alone."

"You get out of my house! Now!"

Mark spun around and stomped out of the apartment, slamming the door behind him.

"And don't come back!" His mother's voice echoed out into the street.

Mark walked and walked until he felt tired enough to sleep. Shivering in the cold, he slipped into an empty basement. Trash and empty cardboard boxes littered the floor. He flattened several of the boxes and spread the cardboard out on the floor. Lying down, he opened several old newspapers and used them as blankets. Still shivering in the cold dampness, he placed cardboard on top of the newspapers. He could hear rats rummaging through the trash. Sleep didn't come that night.

The next day he decided to try to get a job. "At least I'll have money to rent a room," he said to himself.

After going to several places, he was hired as a stock boy at a printing company.

"You can start tomorrow," the manager said. "Be here at 8:30AM."

"Thank you," Mark said.

He thought about going home to tell his mother he had a job, but changed his mind. Instead, he went and got high with some friends. He slept over at one of their houses that night.

The next morning he showed up on time for work, but got high on his lunch hour and didn't return. The following morning he went back to work.

"What are you doing here?" the manager asked.

"I'm here to work," Mark said.

"You go to lunch and don't come back. But now you want to work."

"I'm sorry about that," Mark said. "It won't happen again."

"You're right. It won't happen again. You're fired."

"Come on, man. Give me a break."

"What are you? One of those junkies on the street?"

"I'm not a junkie," Mark said.

"Right. Just get the hell out of here."

Mark left and found some of his friends. They spent the rest of the day getting high.

He went through several jobs in the next few weeks. Finally, he quit looking. Sleeping wherever he could, he often ended up at an apartment with a prostitute. Then, he hooked up with a supplier and started dealing drugs.

One day he was hanging out in a coffee shop when two guys came in. They glanced around, then walked over to Mark.

"You got a 'Spanish quarter'?" the tall one asked.

Mark swung around on his stool and looked at them. He recognized their faces from the general neighborhood.

"What makes you think I got anything?"

"Come on, man. We're lookin' to party."

"You got fifty dollars?"

"Yeah, we got it." They each pulled crumpled bills from their pockets.

"Not here," Mark said. He looked them over again.

Something didn't feel right.

"Well? Where do we go?"

"Come on," Mark said, leading them outside. They walked for about a block. "Wait here," he said.

He returned a short time later with the heroin.

Suddenly, an unmarked cruiser sped down the street, pulling alongside of them. The car stopped, doors swung open, and two narcotic agents swooped down on them.

"Don't move," they warned.

"Well, if it ain't Mutt and Jeff," Mark said. He knew the two detectives. They had tried to bust Mark several times.

"We've got you this time."

"Hey, I don't know what you're talkin' about, man."

"Where is it? Hand it over," they ordered.

"Where's what?"

"You know damn well what." he growled as he slammed Mark up against the car. "I'm in just the right mood to crack a few heads."

One of the two guys Mark was selling the heroin to panicked. "Give it to them, man."

"Shut up!" Mark said.

"Listen to your friend, Mark." the detective said. He still had Mark pinned against the car. "Or I'll rearrange your face."

"He's not my friend," Mark spat out.

"Spread 'em," the detective ordered, starting to frisk Mark. He came to the bulge in Mark's jacket pocket. "Well, well. What have we here?" He pulled out the bag of heroin. "This should put you away for a while," he smirked.

The other agent handcuffed Mark and the other two.

"Get in," he ordered, holding open the door to the back seat. "You have the right to remain silent ..."

All three were found guilty as charged. Mark was sentenced to Rikers Island.

Handcuffed and shackled, Mark was taken from jail and loaded on a bus. He had gone through withdrawal from the heroin while in jail and his mind was clear. A ferry brought the prisoners over to Rikers Island.

Mark looked up at the thick cement walls and solid steel doors.

"Welcome to paradise," an officer said.

Guards with shotguns stood on top of the cement walls surrounding the formidable looking prison. When the steel doors clanged shut behind him, Mark shuddered. He had served time at the reformatory, but this was different. He suddenly felt very alone.

He lined up with the other incoming prisoners to hear the orientation speech. Next they were lined up to get their uniform. Someone whistled at Mark when he was changing his clothes. He looked around. He knew there weren't any women in the room.

"This is trouble," he muttered to himself.

For a short time, he was placed in isolation. When they released him into the general population, he met a lot of inmates he had known from the streets. It was like a reunion. They filled him in on how to handle himself at Riker.

"You stick with your own race here," they warned. "The blacks stick together, the whites stick together, the Spanish stick together."

"Yeah, and don't take any crap from anybody," another said. "And don't show any fear, whether you get whipped or not. If you do, you'll be somebody's 'boy.' "

"Sounds like a great place," Mark said. "Thanks for the warning," he looked around at his friends, "But I can take care of myself."

Mark walked over to the game room. Inmates were hanging out in small groups here and there. Mark picked up a paddle on the ping pong table.

"Hey, Spic. That's mine."

Mark swung around and faced a large black man.

"I don't see your name on it," Mark said, glancing at the paddle, then at the black inmate. "What did you say your name was?"

"I didn't, you mother..."

Mark whacked him across the face with the paddle.

"You s.o.b! I'm going to teach you a lesson." He grabbed Mark around the chest and started squeezing. Mark knew he was in trouble. The black man was much larger than he was. He tried to squirm out of his grasp, but couldn't.

The inmate squeezed tighter. The other inmates quickly formed a circle around them. A good fight always broke up the boredom of their day.

"Kill the Spic," one of the black inmates whispered.

The room grew very quiet. They didn't want to alert the guard who stood just outside the door.

Mark's arms were locked down at his side and the black man had him in a solid bear hug. He managed to twist around just enough to grab the man's groin. He squeezed as hard as he could and didn't let go. Finally, the black man cried out in pain and released Mark.

The guard heard the cry and rushed into the room. Both of them were taken to confinement cells.

Sitting alone on his steel bunk, Mark told himself he'd make sure he never came back to Rikers Island.

"I'd rather get killed than come back here."

Eighteen months had passed since Mark arrived at Rikers Island. This time when the heavy steel doors swung open, he stepped out into freedom.

Going back on the ferry, he started to feel sick. He hadn't been high on drugs for eighteen months. But now, he suddenly craved the heroin again. He needed a fix. When he got off the ferry, he went straight to a connection he knew on the east side of Manhattan and got high.

Then he went to see his mother. She had moved into another neighborhood in Brooklyn while Mark was away.

"Hi," he said, staggering through the door to her apartment. "I'm home."

"Marco," she cried, throwing her arms around him.

"It's good to be home again."

"Let me look at you," she said, stepping back. Her expression changed. "You're high," she said with disgust. "You've only been out for a few hours and you're already high."

"No, you're wrong," Mark said. "I'm not high."

"You'll never change," she said. "You lie, you steal, and you're still a junkie."

"How can you talk to me like that? I'm your son."

"You're no son of mine. You're nothing but a junkie. Get out! I don't have to put up with this."

Mark left and walked down to a nearby nightclub and ordered a drink. Several more drinks followed. He had no place to go.

The piano player started playing "There goes my baby with someone new..."

Mark walked over to the piano and sang along. A small group gathered around him. Several songs later, the club manager came over to him and said, "You've got a good voice.

Maybe I could use you here. What do you say?"

"Are you offering me a job?" Mark asked.

"I'm willing to give you a shot at it. If you can keep my customers drinking, then we've got a deal."

"Sounds okay to me," Mark said, grinning.

He stayed and watched the late show. Angel, one of the dancers, looked real good to him. It had been a while since he had been with a girl. When the show was over, he talked her into letting him go home with her.

The next morning he convinced her to let him stay at her apartment until he got settled. It worked out okay for a while, since they both worked in the same club. But Mark's addiction continued and he wasn't ready for any kind of commitment.

One night after work Mark went to the Apollo Theatre. He met a girl there named Nancy. She was straight, a nice hard-working girl. He started dating her and eventually left Angel to move in with Nancy. She was aware of his drug problem, but thought he would change.

Mark started dealing drugs again to get his own supply of heroin and some extra money. He popped in and out of Nancy's life whenever he felt like it. She got pregnant and had a boy, Mark Junior. She hoped the new baby would settle Mark down.

As time went by an opportunity came up for Mark to do some background singing for Ray Charles, and The Drifters. He was excited about it and Nancy encouraged him to go for it.

"But you need to stop using those drugs," she said. "It'll ruin everything. You could have a whole new career with a chance like this. Don't throw it away."

"Don't you tell me what to do," Mark shouted. "It's my business if I want to get high once in a while."

"Once in a while? Look at yourself. You're a junkie. "

"I'm not a junkie. It's under control. Things couldn't be better right now."

"How can you say that? Look at you. You're a mess."

"Listen, no matter what you think of me, I'm on my way to the top."

"To the top of what?" she said sarcastically.

"I've been trying to tell you the news."

"What news?"

"We're going to be recording with Atlantic Records. McFadden said the contracts are signed."

"Really?"

"Hey, Babe, you're looking at a star." He strutted around her and she laughed in spite of herself. Mark slipped his arms around her.

"You're not lying to me, are you?"

"I wouldn't do that to you," Mark said. "You know I love you."

Nancy sighed. "This could be a chance for us to have a fresh start. Just don't blow it."

A few days later Nancy got a call asking where Mark was. He hadn't shown up for rehearsal again.

"He hasn't been feeling very good," she lied. "But he should be able to be in tomorrow."

"You tell him that he'd better pull himself together. We're getting ready to record and then we're going to California. If he doesn't shape up pretty quick, I'll get a replacement. I don't have time to be fooling around."

"I'll tell him," she said.

Mark didn't come home that night and didn't show up for rehearsal again the next day. Nancy got another phone call.

"Tell him it's over," the manager said. "We don't need him."

A few days later Mark showed up—high.

"Where the hell have you been?" Nancy screamed.

"None of your business." He slipped off his jacket, tossed it on the back of a chair, and walked into the bedroom. "I'm back. That's all that matters."

Nancy followed him into the bedroom.

"Your manager has been calling here looking for you."

"So I missed a few rehearsals. Big deal."

"Big deal? Yeah, it's a big deal. It's all over."

"What are you talking about?"

"It's over. They found someone to replace you. You can't expect them to sit around waiting for you every day."

"Who cares," Mark said, laying down on the bed.

"It's all because of those damn drugs!" she shouted. "You said it was under control."

"I haven't had any stuff for days," he said, closing his eyes. "Now leave me alone. I'm tired."

Nancy stalked out of the room. She snatched his jacket off the back of the chair and searched the pockets. She counted forty-seven joints.

Marching back into the bedroom, she held up a fist full of them. "What do you call these?" she screamed. "You're dealing, aren't you?"

Mark opened his eyes.

"What business do you have going through my pockets?" He got up and walked towards her.

"They're going down the toilet," she said, heading for the bathroom.

Mark caught up with her and jerked her around. "You throw those joints down the toilet and your head goes down there with them." He lowered his voice and Nancy knew it wasn't an idle threat.

She stared at him for a moment, then threw the joints in his face. "That's it," she said. "I can't take any more of this. I'm going to pick up Mark Junior at my mother's. You better be gone when I get back."

"You'll be sorry," Mark said.

She turned and looked at Mark just before closing the door. "And by the way, I'm pregnant again. Not that you give a damn." She slammed the door and left.

Chapter Seven

Over the next few years Mark's addiction got totally out of control. He committed robberies and did some street dealing, but mostly just enough to cover the cost of his own supply of heroin. He slept in the basement of an old apartment building. The superintendent of the building said Mark reminded him of his own son, so he let him stay.

His nights were filled with sleeplessness and nightmares. The basement was dark and damp. It smelled like rotting garbage. Mark had dragged in an old musty mattress from the alley so he'd have something to sleep on. Someone had thrown it out of the third-story window because It had caught on fire. Now the smell of smoke was added to the other odors in the basement. To keep warm, he stole a blanket from a clothesline.

One night as he lay still, trying to get to sleep, he felt something brush across his hair in the darkness. He froze. Then he felt it again. This time around his mouth. It was a rat. His heart pounded and he didn't know what to do. If he moved too quickly, the rat would bite him. He slowly reached down into his pocket, hands trembling. Taking out a book of matches, he struck one of them and it lit up. The rat ran across the floor and scurried under the boiler. Mark ran out of the basement and walked the streets all night. He didn't dare go back down there while it was still dark.

Later that day, he was standing on a street corner with some friends. They were all high. A man wearing a clerical collar was walking towards them.

"Here we go," Mark warned the others. "A fire and brimstone sermon coming up." They laughed and waited for the pastor to come over to them.

"Hello," he said with a friendly smile. "I'm the pastor of the Methodist Church in the neighborhood."

Mark and the others just looked at him, waiting for him to say something about their lifestyle. But he didn't.

"I'd like to invite all of you for dinner at our church," he said.

"What? No lecture?" Mark said.

"Yeah, man. Where's your tracts? Aren't you supposed to try to get us 'saved' or something?"

They all snickered.

"No, actually I just wanted to invite you to dinner. I thought you might enjoy a good hearty meal. It's Saturday night at six o'clock. I hope you'll come." He turned and walked back down the sidewalk.

"Hey, Mark. I think his church is the one where all the rich snobs go. You know, furs, jewelry..." He had a mischievous grin on his face.

"Ooohee," the other one said. "I feel hungry already."

They all laughed.

When Saturday night came, they decided to go to the church. It was rare for them to get a decent meal, especially Mark. They swaggered into the building, trying to look cool. The aroma of home-cooked food filled the air. "Let's get in line," Mark said, motioning towards the buffet.

They filled their plates and sat down at one of the long tables. A young man came over to their table.

"Welcome, brother," he said to Mark. "Glad you came."

"Yeah, thanks," Mark said. He continued to eat.

"I want to show you something." he said.

Mark looked up.

He lifted his shirt and said to Mark, "See all these scars? I was a junkie and a rip-off artist for years. But Jesus changed all that. Now I'm free, healthy and happy."

Mark stared at him. "You've got to be kidding me," he said.

"It's true," he said. "Jesus changed my life."

"Right," Mark said. He shoved the last bite of food in his mouth, got up, and left. His friends followed.

"What a bunch of jive." Mark said when they got outside.

"At least the food was good," his friend said, rubbing his stomach with pleasure.

They all laughed.

It was cold outside and Mark headed for his spot in the basement. He dragged his soiled mattress over next to the boiler to keep warm. But not without checking underneath for rats first. Pulling his dirty blanket over him, he fell asleep quickly for the first time in weeks.

He had been asleep for quite a while when something woke him. He heard footsteps coming down to the basement. He scrambled off the mattress and hid behind the boiler. Sometimes the police checked the basements for junkies to bust. On cold winter nights like this, they usually got a few. No one was out on the streets. They'd freeze to death.

He watched a shadowy figure pass the boiler and go into the next room. Whoever it was, carried a large paper bag. Mark quietly slipped out from behind the boiler and followed him in the darkness.

The stranger placed the paper bag on the floor and began pulling out candles, one by one. He placed them in a circle on the floor and then lit each one. When all the flames flickered in the dark room, he stepped into the center of the circle of candles and suddenly began wailing and praying to Satan.

It gave Mark the creeps. He felt a weird, evil presence in the room and got scared. He slowly backed away from the doorway and then dashed up the steps and out into the street. It was cold and daylight had already broken. He ran and ran until he thought his heart would burst through his chest. He ended up in front of the church where he and his friends had dinner the night before.

Well-dressed people were arriving at the church for the early morning service. Cold and shivering, Mark walked inside. He peered into the sanctuary with its bright red carpeting and large pipe organ. A cross hung over the platform. Something was wrong with it. He stared at it for a minute. Jesus wasn't on it. It was empty. In the Catholic church, Christ always was on the cross.

He heard a voice inside him saying, "Get out of here. Get out now. Nobody in here cares about you. You're nothing but a dirty junkie."

Then he looked around. People glanced awkwardly at him and then looked away. His clothes were torn and filthy and he smelled. He couldn't remember the last time he had a bath. Embarrassed, he quickly sat down in the back pew. No one sat near him.

The voice inside Mark's head repeated, "Get out of here. You don't belong here. Look at you. Who cares about you?"

Mark started to get up to leave, but then remembered how cold it was outside. He didn't want to go back to that basement right now. He settled back into the pew.

The pastor got up and led the singing, followed by a brief sermon. Mark felt the pastor's words were directed at him. It made him angry. When the service was over, the pastor came over to Mark and said, "I know a person who can help solve your problems. His name is Jesus Christ."

Mark looked at him standing there in his long flowing robe with stripes on the sleeves.

"How in the world can you stand there and tell me that Jesus can solve my problems?" Mark didn't attempt to hide the anger in his voice. "Have you ever been so hungry that you thought you would die? Have you ever been spit on just because you're a 'Spic'? Have you ever done time in the joint? How dare you stand there and say to me, 'Jesus is the answer.' You don't know what you're talking about, man."

People were still milling around talking and visiting. They all grew very quiet at Mark's outburst.

"I haven't experienced those things," the pastor said in a kind voice. "But Jesus has."

Mark stared at him. He didn't know what to say.

"Here," the pastor said, reaching into his pocket. He handed Mark a five dollar bill.

Mark glanced around at all the people staring. He grabbed the money and ran out of the church. He used it to buy some smack, went back to the basement, and got high.

All day the pastor's words haunted him.

"Jesus is the answer."

Restless, he tossed and turned all night. How did I get to this point? Filthy, dirty, sleeping in basements. He had to face the facts. He was a junkie. He couldn't deny it anymore. He still didn't understand how Jesus could be the answer. But the words echoed in his head all night. Not able to sleep, he finally just lay still waiting for daylight. Early the next morning, he walked back over to the church. He found the pastor in his office.

"I need help," Mark said.

The pastor smiled. "That's the first step," he said. "I know a place where you can get the kind of help you need. It's a program called Teen Challenge. Are you willing to go?"

"Yes, I'll go," Mark said. All the anger had subsided. He just felt helpless and alone.

"I must warn you, it's a religious program," the pastor said. "They'll be talking a lot about Jesus."

"I don't care, " Mark said. "I'll go anywhere."

Chapter Eight

Mark stepped into the Teen Challenge building and heard voices singing, "There is power, power, wonder working power..."

For a moment he hesitated. The atmosphere was more like a church than a drug rehabilitation program. The pastor had told him it was a religious program. He couldn't turn back now.

He was ushered into David Wilkerson's office. David got up from his chair, came around the desk and shook Mark's hand with a firm grasp. He looked directly into Mark's eyes and asked, "Do you really want help?"

It made Mark nervous. He felt this guy could read his mind.

"Yes, I want help," Mark said. He tried to sound confident. "What are you going to give me to help kick this habit?"

"We aren't going to give you anything," David grinned. "But someone will stay with you at all times and will pray you through."

"Cold turkey? No medication?"

"That's right."

Mark panicked for a minute. He'd been through withdrawal once in jail and it wasn't a pleasant experience. Now his habit was a lot worse.

"Having second thoughts?" David asked.

"Well, no, I really don't have any choice."

"Good," David said. "Now, let's pray together and then one of our staff members will help you get settled."

Mark took a shower and was given clean clothes. Then there were the clean sheets on a clean bed. It felt good. Until withdrawal began. For the next few days, Mark got so sick that he thought he was going to die. He had hallucinations, felt like bugs were crawling all over his skin, vomited, and had screaming and crying spells. A staff member stayed by his side the whole time.

"I know it's hard, Mark. But hang in there. You'll make it. I did it and you can too. Just remember that God loves you. I'm going to pray for you now."

On the fifth day, he rested comfortably for the first time. He stretched out in bed and realized he actually felt good. A staff member tapped on Mark's door.

"It's time for chapel, Mark."

Chapel? That was the last place he wanted to go. But he reminded himself that at least he had three square meals a day and a clean bed to sleep in. He'd better go along with the program.

He got up, showered and dressed, and went downstairs to the chapel. When he stepped into the room, men were on their knees, praying. There seemed to be a glowing presence in the room. Mark shook his head, thinking he was just hallucinating. But it was still there.

One of the staff stood up and said, "I want to read John 3:16 to you."

" 'For God so loved the world, that He gave His only begotten Son, that whosoever believeth in Him should not perish, but have everlasting life.' "

"It doesn't matter who you are or what you've done. God is saying here that He loves you. You are a person of value and He has a special plan for your life."

"Jesus wants you to respond to His love and dedicate your life to Him. I'm not talking about joining a church or a denomination. I'm talking about a personal relationship with the Son of God. He can be your closest friend. Someone you can trust. Someone who loves you, no matter what."

Mark felt the love in the room. This wasn't what he had expected. He thought there would be a lecture on rules and regulations. And here someone was standing in front of him, saying that God loved him. It was almost too much for him.

"What have you to lose if you give your life to Christ? Unhappiness, for one thing, and loneliness and emptiness. And what will you gain by giving your life to Christ? Feeling loved, fulfilled. You'll experience joy and have a sense of purpose for your life. Why don't you come forward and lay your sins and your problems at the altar? God will forgive you and give you a fresh start."

He got out of his seat and went to the altar.

"God, please help me," he sobbed.

Several men gathered around him and began praying for him. Mark cried. For the first time, the tears didn't seem to be a sign of weakness. He felt a release, a cleansing taking place within. When he got up off his knees, he was a new person. Everything seemed new.

Over the next few weeks Mark read his Bible over and over. He liked the story of the Apostle Peter.

"Always getting into trouble with that mouth of his," Mark chuckled. "I can relate to that."

Then he read the account of Peter's denial of Jesus before the Crucifixion. He put the Bible down for a minute and wondered if he'd do the same thing. How would he handle telling his old friends about the change in him? What if they made fun of him? Would he deny Christ? The questions bothered him.

He picked up his Bible again and continued reading. He read about Peter getting baptized in the Holy Spirit. That experience changed Peter's life. He had a new boldness in speaking to others about Jesus. Mark closed his Bible and slipped to his knees.

"Lord, if that experience Peter had in the Upper Room was real, then that's what I need in my life. I need something I can touch and feel. I need the Baptism of the Holy Spirit." Mark knelt in silence for a while, not sure what he was waiting for. Nothing happened.

Several weeks went by and he began to think about leaving the program. He got frustrated with the regimented schedule. After all, he reasoned, I'm an adult. I don't need someone to tell me what to do every day.

One morning he packed up his things before going down to breakfast. He planned to leave at the end of the day. He went downstairs and checked the schedule on the wall. He had kitchen duty.

He helped prepare breakfast and then started on the dishes. A guest speaker was there to speak in chapel that morning. Mark didn't want to miss out on anything and kept slipping out of the kitchen into the doorway of the chapel to listen.

"Mark," It was another staff member. "You've got to stay in the kitchen and get your work done. We've got forty-five guys for lunch today. If you keep coming out here, it'll never be ready on time."

"Okay," Mark sighed and went back to the kitchen.

At lunch time the speaker walked over to Mark, looked him in the eye, and said, "Can I pray for you?"

Surprised, Mark said, "Sure."

"Come with me to the chapel."

Mark followed him.

"I sense that God wants to do something special for you today," he said. "Just kneel here in His presence for a while. Praise Him and thank Him for what He's done in your life."

Mark obeyed and began praising God. After a few minutes, he felt God's presence in the room. He had never experienced anything quite like this before. It was like liquid love. He opened his mouth to continue praising. What came out was not English or Spanish. He spoke in tongues. God had given him a prayer language. Excited, Mark didn't want to stop. He just prayed and prayed. He was afraid it might not come back if he stopped. Then he realized what had happened. He had received the Baptism of the Holy Spirit. The very thing he had prayed for earlier. He felt wonderful. Then he remembered that he had packed his things to leave. He chuckled to himself; God had stopped him in His own way.

A new hunger for reading the Bible and for wanting to reach out and share with others grew within him. He decided to commit to Teen Challenge's one year training program at their farm in Pennsylvania.

When he completed that year, he returned to New York and spent another year working with the Teen Challenge program in Brooklyn. He worked as staff during the day and at night he attended a Spanish Bible College.

He began to go out speaking at churches, representing Teen Challenge and sharing his testimony. The new Christian friendships he formed were so different from what he had experienced in the past. He was excited about his faith and thought every other Christian felt the same way. But he soon discovered that wasn't so. An experience in a southern church was about to challenge his thinking.

Mark had been looking forward to visiting this particular church. They had been good financial supporters of the ministry. Mark wanted to thank them and to let them know that the money they had donated was bearing fruit. Lives were being changed.

As his custom, he arrived at the church early in order to spend some time in personal prayer before the service began. He walked towards the front and sat at the end of a pew.

People slowly started drifting in for the service. Mark remained seated. Different ones glanced over at him, then sat at some distance. One woman came down the aisle, planning to sit in the row Mark was in. She looked at the tattoo of an eagle and a rose on Mark's arm. Mark smiled at her. Embarrassed, she quickly looked away and then found a seat in another part of the sanctuary.

"I guess they're not used to speakers with tattoos," Mark said to himself. He chuckled. Then his thoughts drifted back to when he got the tattoo. It was on Coney Island. He was stoned and decided to let 'Frankenstein' give him a tattoo. At the time, he figured it might help cover the needle tracks on his arms. Besides, it was macho to have a tattoo. His father had a big Indian on his arm, an American Eagle spread out on his chest, and a variety of things all over his back. As a kid, Mark thought that was the sign of a 'real man'. Mark sighed, thinking how wrong he had been about so many things.

People continued to fill the church. And they continued to avoid sitting near Mark. Then he overheard a whispered comment about a nigger in the church. Being Spanish, Mark had dark skin. With a suntan on top of it, he could almost pass for a black person. But so what? What was wrong with these people? Christians shouldn't have that kind of prejudice. He began steaming inside. How can they praise God with their 'hallelujahs' in one breath, and then mumble nigger with their next breath? Even the pastor avoided Mark at first, not realizing who he was. Mark heard him comment to someone that he thought the speaker would be here by now. He continued to shake hands throughout the church and finally came to where Mark was sitting.

"Hello," he said. "I'm Pastor Smith. Can I help you with something?"

"I'm here for the service," Mark said.

"Oh, yes. Of course." The pastor cleared his throat.

"I'm your speaker," Mark said through clenched teeth.

"Oh, praise God!" the pastor shouted, pumping Mark's hand up and down. "Thank you, Jesus. Hallelujah."

"What a phony," Mark thought.

The pastor led the congregation in a few songs and then introduced Mark.

Mark walked slowly to the podium, collecting his thoughts. He stood and looked out at the congregation in silence for a moment. They grew uncomfortable.

"I want to share a little story with you," Mark began. "A little black boy sat, crying, on the front steps of a big church. Jesus came and sat next to the little boy, putting His arm around the boy's shoulders."

" 'Son, why are you crying?' Jesus asked."

" 'Sir,' the little boy sobbed, 'they won't let me in their church.' "

" 'Don't worry, son,' Jesus said, as He held the boy close. 'They won't let me in either.' "

Mark let his point sink in. People grew restless in the silence. After a few moments, he continued on and shared his own testimony of how God had changed his life—the life of a junkie.

Later, Mark shared this experience with another staff member. Still angry about the incident, Mark said to his friend, "I wish Teen Challenge would tell this group to rub their money in their chest. Do they realize the prejudice that's in that church?"

"Mark, calm down," his friend said. "These people have been good supporters for many years. Yes, you're right. They're prejudiced. They're not perfect."

"I'd like to expose those turkeys for what they really are," Mark continued. "They remind me of the people in Revelations that said, 'Didn't we do this in Your name and that in Your name?' And Jesus said to them, 'you workers of iniquity, I never knew you.' "

"Remember, the Bible also says, 'Vengeance is mine.' "

"Yeah, I know," Mark said. "I'm just so angry. I guess I need to pray about my own attitude."

"Uh-huh," his friend smiled at him.

As Mark worked through the fact that there are phony Christians, and imperfect Christians, God began to deal with him about his own relationships, especially with his parents. One morning he felt God say to him that he should go talk with his mother. He had to forgive her for her neglect and the times she had hurt him; and he had to ask for forgiveness for his own behavior. He obeyed that inner voice.

He went to visit her and they said some honest, hard things to each other. It was the beginning of a healing process in their relationship. She told Mark things that he hadn't realized. And he shared with her his new faith in Christ. It was a good visit. He began to pray for his brother, Raphael, who was running with a gang and had ended up serving time in prison.

Mark also wanted to speak to his father, whom he guessed was still in Puerto Rico. Now age 27, Mark hadn't seen his father in many years. He made no effort to track him down, but began praying about it every day.

One day a letter arrived at Teen Challenge for Mark. It was from his father! Mark wondered how his father found him. He invited Mark to come visit him. So Mark made the arrangements and left for Puerto Rico.

His father was friendly at first. Mark told him about the change in his life, his faith in God, and about Teen Challenge.

"That's fine," he said to Mark. "I'm glad you're doing okay. But I don't want any of those religious fanatics around me. Just don't bug me about it."

That day Mark was riding a bus in Puerto Rico and recognized one of the passengers. It was a young man who had been through the Teen Challenge program in New York. Excited to see each other, they spent some time sharing what had happened in their lives. Mark invited him to come meet his father.

When they went to the house, Mark introduced him to his father and told him he had gone through the Teen Challenge program, too. The three of them chatted a while and then his friend left.

"Come into my room," Mark's father said. Mark sensed something was wrong.

As soon as they were in the bedroom, Mark's father punched him right in the face. Mark tumbled to the floor.

"How dare you defy me!" he shouted at Mark. "I told you not to bring any of those religious people around here." He was working himself into a rage.

For a moment, Mark flashed back to scenes of his childhood when his father beat his mother. His natural instinct was to get up and settle things once and for all. He knew he could beat his father. He slowly stood up, rubbing his jaw.

His father ran out of the room and Mark heard a female voice screaming, "No...no!"

His father's wife came running to Mark. "Get out of the house. Quick. He's got a knife. He said he's going to kill you. Your father is crazy!"

Mark hesitated briefly, but decided to leave. Turning the other cheek was the hardest thing for him to do.

A short time later, back in New York, Mark received a letter from his father asking for forgiveness. He asked Mark to pray for Raphael and he told him that one of his half-brothers was also a Christian, a missionary. Mark realized that God's way is always the best way.

Chapter Nine

Mark began to feel restless at Teen Challenge. Good things were happening, but he felt it was time for him to move on to something else.

"If God is calling you to move," a friend said, "then He'll make it clear. Just be patient."

The following week Mark had a dream. He saw himself traveling in a car, passing corn fields and cows. It reminded him of an earlier trip he had made to the Ohio State Fair. He had gone there to witness to the kids at the fair. While there, he stayed with Mrs. Pane, a Christian lady. He enjoyed the Christian fellowship while there, but didn't like being in the country. He was a city boy. He'd be happy if he never saw another cow in his entire life.

For three nights in a row Mark had this same dream about traveling past corn fields and cows. He tried to pass it off as just another dream, but couldn't. Perhaps God was speaking to him through the dream.

He wrote a letter to Mrs. Pane in Columbus. He shared with her that he felt ready to leave Teen Challenge and move on to something else, but wasn't sure of God's direction. A few days later he received a telegram.

COME TO COLUMBUS.
WE'RE STARTING A MINISTRY,
CAN USE YOUR HELP.

He said good-bye to his friends on the Teen Challenge staff and headed for Columbus, Ohio.

"Please don't put me out in the country near any cows." Mark prayed as he drove.

A man named Victor had just started a store-front street ministry. Mark moved into the store-front and spent his time talking with kids on the streets, counseling and witnessing. He enjoyed the ministry, but felt frustrated at times over not having any spending money. Then he met a Christian businessman who asked him to work as a Sales Trainee.

Feeling that it was an answer to prayer, Mark accepted the position. He looked forward to having a regular paycheck and feeling like a 'normal' working person. Just before starting the job, someone else approached Mark about starting a ministry for kids in Newark, Ohio.

"I just accepted a job," Mark said. "I can't just quit before I even get started. It wouldn't be right."

"Pray about it," the man said. "I've seen the results of your work and I really believe you're the one to do it."

Mark didn't feel he needed to pray about it. He had already made his decision. He was going to work a normal job and be a normal person.

He moved out of the store-front and into a house near Ohio State University. Mrs. Pace had purchased it to be used for campus ministry. Mark worked during the day and continued his ministry at night. He held Bible studies and fellowship meetings for the college students and maintained his contact with the street people.

On Saturday he walked the streets of Columbus, witnessing and talking with kids. A drunk girl bumped into him, stumbling along the sidewalk.

"Do you know that Jesus loves you?" Mark asked. She stopped, stared at him for a minute and tried to focus her eyes.

"Do you need help?" Mark asked.

She spit in his face.

Mark wiped off the spittle with his handkerchief as the girl continued on down the street, weaving and stumbling.

"Lord, reach out and touch her," Mark whispered.

That night Mark held a meeting for street people. A young woman walked in, dressed like a man. Mark walked over to her and said, "Jesus loves you. We're glad you came."

She just stared at him.

He wondered whether to brace himself to be spit at again. But the girl just stood there, her dark eyes glaring.

"Would you mind if I prayed for you?" Mark asked.

She didn't respond.

Mark motioned for her to sit down in a nearby chair. He sat next to her. First he prayed for her, then he began talking, trying to get her to open up. "You really don't have to continue the lifestyle you're living," he said. "You look unhappy. God can give you a fresh start."

Her eyes sparked with anger for a moment, then she regained control.

"Would you pray for me one more time?" she asked. Her eyes remained cold and her voice unnatural.

"Of course," Mark said. He closed his eyes and bowed his head.

As soon as he did, the girl slipped a knife out of her purse and lunged at Mark. He felt the movement and opened his eyes. She swung the knife toward his stomach, but it didn't penetrate. She raised her hand over her head to strike again with the knife. Mark put his arm up for protection. The sharp blade slashed his arm and he began to bleed.

"I'm going to kill you," she said. Her voice was husky and troubled.

A friend of Mark's saw the commotion and dashed across the room, grabbing the girl from behind.

"I'll kill you, too," she said, trying to squirm out his grasp.

Mark forced the knife out of her hand.

"You must be hurting pretty bad to pull something like this," Mark said. His voice was calm and soothing.

Her hard look softened and she burst into tears. "I don't know what came over me," she said.

"It's okay. Just calm down and let's talk."

At that point Mark's friend released his grip on her. The three of them talked for a long time. She poured out her problems and Mark shared his testimony with her. Before she left, she prayed and asked God to take control of her life.

"One thing's for sure," Mark said to his friend when they were leaving. "Anyone who says being a Christian is boring doesn't know what they're talking about."

They looked at each other and laughed.

"We'd better tend to that cut of yours," his friend said. He checked Mark's arm. Mark had wrapped a clean handkerchief around the cut. "It doesn't look too bad." He grinned at Mark. "It's all part of ministry."

"Yeah, easy for you to say," Mark mumbled. "I'm the one with the battle scars."

Shortly after Mark started his new job, his boss called him into his office.

"I need to talk to you, Mark. I'm leaving the company. I really feel God is telling me to start my own business. That's going to mean a change for you, too. I can't afford to hire anyone right away. But the management here has agreed to keep you on. They'll have to move you to another division. I'm afraid that means a cut in pay."

"Well," Mark sighed, "maybe this is God's way of speaking to me about ministry."

"What do you mean?"

"I've been asked to go to Newark, Ohio and get back into full-time ministry. I've been fighting it."

"I'll be praying for you. If it's God, He won't let you off the hook."

"I know."

A few weeks later, Mark left for Newark, wondering what God had in store for him there.

A Methodist church sponsored the ministry in Newark. They purchased a large home in a location where street people could drop in, and they called it Chiros House.

Mark's voice and footsteps echoed through the empty rooms the first day he moved in. For the first time, he felt lonely. He was used to having a lot of people around. He spent extra time in prayer and Bible reading, preparing for the ministry God had for him. Those first few weeks in the house he often felt as though he was alone in a monastery.

He went out into the streets, but at first didn't get much response. Then one day there was a knock on the door that changed everything.

Mark opened the door and faced a young man, body trembling, eyes glazed. Mark recognized the symptoms. He was coming off LSD.

"I need help," he said. Tremors shook his body.

"Come on in," Mark said. He led him into the living room. "What's your name?"

"Gary," he mumbled. "Gary Green." He glanced nervously around the room. His eyes stopped at the large wooden cross hanging on one wall.

"Come and sit down, Gary. Let's talk. Tell me what's been going on in your life."

Gary sank into a chair and started talking. His thoughts were disconnected. Whenever he seemed to be running out of something to talk about, Mark encouraged him to continue and kept him occupied, talking for three hours.

"I'm going to pray for you now, Gary."

Gary looked at Mark, then glanced over at the cross again.

Mark placed his hands on Gary's head. "In the Name of Jesus, I command you to take your hands off this young man, Satan."

Gary's eyes widened. His body shuddered, then quieted.

"I need to go upstairs to the restroom for a minute," Mark said. "You stay here. I'll be right back down. You're going to be okay."

When Mark returned, Gary had curled up at the foot of the cross and was sound asleep on the floor. The tremors had stopped. An acid trip usually lasted about 12 hours. Gary had come down in three.

Gary slept peacefully for a long time. When he woke up, he asked Mark what happened. Mark shared about Jesus and what He could do in Gary's life. Gary listened, prayed and asked God to take control of his life then went outside, walking up and down the street, telling others what happened to him when Mark prayed.

Over the next few weeks more and more kids from the street came to Chiros House and Mark's little prayer meeting soon mushroomed to 125. Many got saved and delivered from drug and alcohol addiction. Some went back to school, some into ministry training, some to work. Their lives had changed and it showed.

Miracles continued and Mark's life was busy. He was truly in the midst of a revival. But that nagging loneliness remained with him. He began to pray for a companion.

"Lord, I'm busy. I don't have much time for dating. Just bring me a wife."

A short time later, Becky contacted Mark. She had heard him speak in her church. Although she came from a stable Christian home, she had gotten involved in a destructive lifestyle. Impressed with Mark's testimony, she came to him for help.

After they talked for a while, Mark asked her what she felt her biggest problem was.

"I just never felt accepted by my father," she said. "He wanted a son, but got stuck with me."

"What's important is that you're accepted by God," Mark said. "He loves you just the way you are."

Her big blue eyes filled with tears.

"You don't know the things I've done—the way I've lived," she said. Tears slowly found their way down her cheeks.

"It couldn't be any worse than the things I've done," Mark said, "and God accepts me." He reached out and took Becky's hands in his. "Let me pray for you."

After Mark prayed, Becky wept, rocking back and forth. "God, forgive me." she said over and over again.

When the tears stopped, she looked up at Mark. "Thank you," she said.

"It's the Lord, not me," Mark said.

She gave Mark a hug and left. That night before going to bed, Mark prayed for Becky and then prayed for himself. He was concerned about the way he felt when she hugged him. He felt attracted to her.

Over the next weeks Becky continued to come to Mark for counseling. During that time the attraction between them grew. Although she had many emotional problems to work through, Mark felt Becky was the answer to his prayer for a wife. Now that she had accepted the Lord, he saw no reason to wait. They got married and Becky became involved in the ministry. She had a deep compassion for those who came to Chiros House and it seemed as though Mark had made the right choice. But many of the problems from Becky's past lifestyle began to surface.

Mark couldn't understand it. When he got saved, his whole life changed and he had no desire to go back to his old ways. Why would anyone look back after they made a commitment to follow Jesus? He tried to reason with her, but she got more and more restless and irritable. One day when he came back from a speaking engagement, she was gone.

Several weeks later she came back, acting as though everything was fine.

"Where have you been?"

"I don't want to talk about it."

"You're my wife. I have a right to know."

"I'm back. Isn't that enough?"

"No, it's not enough. Becky, we have a ministry here. What kind of an example is this to the others?"

"That's your problem, not mine."

This discussion took place many times over the next few years. Becky would just disappear for a few days or a week. Several times Mark went out looking for her and found her in a bar. She finally admitted to having an affair. Each time she came back with the promise of not doing it again.

One night he got down on his knees, crying out to God.

"Lord, you know I don't believe in divorce, but I can't live like this. If I go out, I never know if she's going to be here when I get back. I know she's seeing someone else. I'd rather give up the ministry than go on like this, or to be a stumbling block to someone."

The next day Mark went to a friend for personal counsel. He poured his heart out, sharing what had been going on for the past two years.

"It's so hard," Mark said. "We're in the midst of a revival, with people getting saved and healed, and yet my own marriage is failing. Maybe I need to just quit the ministry."

"Mark, you know God has called you to minister. Look at the results. There should be no question in your mind about that."

Mark sighed. "I sure don't feel very 'called' at this moment."

"Listen, what you probably need is a rest. You've been too busy. Why don't you just get away by yourself for a while and get a new perspective on things. Listen to what God is saying to you."

"You're right. I do need to get away for a while. I need to sort things out."

"And Mark—I'm not saying that you shouldn't get a divorce. You've got a Biblical right to do that. But you need a clear head about it. You need to be sure."

"I know." Mark stood to leave. "Thanks, brother. I appreciate your help."

"That's what friends are for."

Mark took a leave of absence from the ministry and went to the Teen Challenge farm in Pennsylvania. As he spent the first few weeks unwinding, he struggled with whether he ever wanted to go back to ministry. He didn't like the pressure of being in the public eye all the time. There wasn't any privacy to work out his own personal problems.

He walked alone through the fields at the farm and poured his heart out before God. Most of what came out were negative feelings and frustrations with his marriage. When he got all those out, he thought about the kids on the streets. He thought about the Gary Greens. That's what kept him going. Hurting kids, scared kids, kids who were strung out on drugs and alcohol as an escape from their negative environment. He knew how they felt and he cared—he cared a lot.

One Sunday a visitor attending one of the services at Teen Challenge came over to Mark.

"I remember you," she said. "You spoke at our church in Chillicothe, Ohio a few years ago. Your testimony had quite an impact on our youth."

"Praise God for that," Mark said.

"What are you doing now?"

"I'm taking a 'sabbatical', " Mark said. "I needed a rest."

"Then what?"

"I'm really not sure."

"Well, praise God." She smiled at Mark. "I've got something for you to consider. A pastor in our community is trying to start a youth ministry and he's looking for help. Someone to head it up."

"I don't know."

"At least come and talk to him. If you don't take the position, at least you could give him some advice on how to get it off the ground. You've had the kind of experience he's looking for."

"Let me think about it," Mark said.

"You do that. And pray about it. Who knows, maybe God placed me here today just to speak to you." She grinned at Mark.

"I suppose it wouldn't hurt to check it out," Mark said.

"Great. I'll let the pastor know you're coming." She shook Mark's hand and left after giving him a phone number to call.

Mark went to Chillicothe and met with a Presbyterian pastor.

"The church is solidly behind this outreach," he said. "Right now we're looking for a house where we can locate the ministry."

"What is your goal, your main purpose for this ministry?" Mark asked.

"We want to reach the youth of the community. We're concerned about them and the drug problem. We need someone like you to head this up. Someone who understands them, who can talk their language. I feel you're that person."

"I've been praying for God's direction," Mark said.

"The community is behind us too. The mayor is on the board of directors and the city treasurer will oversee the finances. We've checked into some grants that are available for drug rehabilitation programs. It's all coming together. You can live in the ministry house and we'll pay you a weekly salary. You won't have to be concerned about raising funds. Others will do that for you."

"It sounds really good," Mark said. "Give me a few days and I'll let you know for sure."

Mark discussed the move with Becky and she said it sounded good to her.

"Are you sure you want to go?" Mark asked.

"Why? Don't you want me to?"

"I didn't say that," Mark said. "It's just that..." He sighed. "Maybe the change of location will be good for both of us. A fresh start."

He called the pastor in Chillicothe and accepted the position.

Chapter Ten

"I think we've found just the right house," Pastor White said to Mark. "It's on top of a hill in a very nice part of town."

"Are you sure the people in the 'nice' part of town will want to have street people living near them?"

"Believe me, it won't be a problem. You'll like it. It's a 14 room house surrounded by 27 acres of beautiful land."

"It sounds good. You're sure it won't be a problem to that neighborhood?"

"I'm sure. You see, the house was the living quarters for the nurses who worked in the local sanitarium. It's closed down now. I want you to drive over and see what you think."

Mark and Becky drove over to the house. When Mark stepped inside the front door, he stood across from a winding carved wooden staircase leading up to the second floor. From the window at the top of the stairs, a shard of bright sunlight pierced the darkness of the house. The warmth of it fell on Mark's face.

"This is the place," he said to Becky. "I can feel it."

They roamed from room to room.

"It's huge," Becky said.

"We'll be able to take in a lot of people," Mark said. "God must have something big in mind."

"What about furniture?" Becky asked. "Everything we own could fit into one room."

"For now we'll just have to live with what we've got. If we can get someone to donate mattresses, we can just put them on the floor until we get beds. If the people in the community are really behind this, then they'll help with the furniture. And we can check out some used furniture shops. It'll be exciting watching it all come together."

"Yeah, exciting," Becky mumbled.

Mark looked at her, but didn't react. He knew she hadn't been feeling well lately. She was tired all the time. They walked back outside.

"What's that building next door?" she asked. "It looks like a hospital."

"It's a mental health clinic now," Mark said. "It used to be part of a sanitarium."

"How appropriate."

"I'm glad they're up here," Mark said. "This way we won't have any zoning problems using the house for rehabilitation." They walked around the grounds.

"On the other side of the hill is the Chillicothe Campus of Ohio State University." Mark pointed. "All this surrounding land belongs to them. It's really beautiful up here."

"Yes, it is," Becky admitted. "It's a great place to start a family."

Mark looked at her in surprise.

"I'm pregnant," she said. "We're going to have a baby."

"Is that why you haven't been feeling well lately?"

"Apparently. Are you happy about it?"

"Of course I am," he said. "I just wasn't expecting it. It's a good thing I'm getting a weekly salary." He laughed, but then grew quiet.

"What's the matter?"

"I was just thinking about my other two kids. Wondering where they are. How they're doing."

"Two kids? You just mentioned one—Mark Junior."

"Nancy was pregnant when she left me. I was such a mess back then. I had no idea how to be a father."

"All that has changed now. I have a feeling you'll be a very good father."

"I didn't exactly have a positive role model to follow with my own father," Mark said "But I know better now. This kid will know his father loves him."

"What if it's a girl?" She thought of her own father's disappointment in having a girl instead of a boy.

"It doesn't really matter," Mark said. "I'm just glad to have another chance at being a father."

They walked back to their car hand in hand. Mark suddenly stopped. "I know what I'm going to name the house," he said.

"What?"

"Anchor House."

"I like it."

"We'll provide an anchor for people's souls. People who are being tossed around by all the problems in their lives—drugs, alcohol, abuse. We'll let them know that Jesus is the anchor that can still that storm inside of them." He felt a new enthusiasm as he spoke the words.

"Sounds like a sermon coming on," Becky teased.

"I'm ready to start again," he said. "It feels good. I'm going to get out into this community and get to know the people. And let them get to know me. God is going to perform miracles here."

"He already has," Becky said. She put her arms around Mark.

They settled into the house and Mark began speaking in the local schools and churches. He shared with them what God had done in his life and his burden for reaching others.

"Our doors at Anchor House are always open," he said. "If you know of someone who is hurting and needs a place to stay, he is welcome in our home."

Within a few days someone from the mental health clinic next door came over to talk with Mark.

"I have someone who needs a place to live," he said.

"I'd be glad to talk with him," Mark said. "Bring him over and let's discuss it. I'll help in any way I can."

"Well, maybe you'd better let me tell you a little about him first."

"Okay."

"As you know, the governor has pushed for an investigation of the mental health system. As a result, we've discovered a number of people that really don't belong in the state hospital. They just got lost in the system somehow and now we're trying to place them somewhere. Don is one of them."

"How can someone get 'lost' in the system?"

"Don's story is a bit unique. According to the limited records we found, Don's parents were killed in a car accident when he was about nine years old. He lost his hearing in that accident and was put into the state hospital for observation. Because no family ever claimed him, he just got left there. It's been 22 years."

"Twenty-two years? How could that happen? Why didn't he speak up?"

"That's just it. He can't talk or hear. He's a deaf mute."

"Twenty-two years in an institution? Is he okay? How does he communicate?"

"He's very adept at sign language."

"I don't know anything about sign language. But I suppose I could learn."

"He knows how to write."

"Well, then I guess we'll be able to communicate," Mark said. "I'd like to meet him."

"I knew you would." He smiled at Mark. "He's out in the car. I'll get him."

Don stepped inside, glanced at Mark, then shuffled past him into the house. He walked slowly around the living room, absorbing everything. He read the posters hanging on the walls. Then he turned and grinned at Mark.

Mark grinned back.

Don reached into his pocket and pulled out a small card. He shoved it into Mark's palm.

Mark read it. It said, "I'm a born-again Christian." Mark looked at Don's face. He was grinning at Mark, nodding his head up and down. Then he grabbed Mark's hand and began pumping his arm up and down, grinning the whole time. He acted like he had found a long-lost friend.

"I'll take him," Mark said through misted eyes.

Don gathered his few personal belongings from the car and was released to Mark. When they were alone, Don pulled another card out of his pocket.

"I know," Mark said. "You're a born-again Christian." Don grinned mischievously and forced the card into Mark's hand. Mark started to put the card in his pocket, but Don grabbed it. He held it up, pointed at Mark, then at the card.

"Okay, okay," Mark chuckled. "I'll read it."

"I love blondes"!

Don stood, bobbing his head up and down, his eyes sparkling in delight.

Mark roared with laughter.

"We're going to get along just fine," Mark said, giving him a bear hug.

Don settled into the house and Mark soon discovered what an asset he was. He loved to work in the yard and clean up around the house. Mark told him he had the official job of Maintenance Man. Proud of his new title, Don kept the place in good shape.

A short time later a reporter from a local newspaper came out to Anchor House and interviewed Mark. After the article appeared in the paper, the calls began pouring in. Within weeks the house was full and humming with activities.

There were Bible studies, fellowship meetings and mini-concerts. Many drug-addicted youth came to Mark for help and he used all the training he got at Teen Challenge to work with them. He began holding Sunday worship services at the house for those who didn't fit into the traditional church. The services vibrated with the music of Christian bands and ended with ministry and prayer for those in need. Some people showed up just out of curiosity; some just to hear the music.

A drummer from a local band came to one of the mini-concerts at the house. 'The Happy Pigs' were performing. They picked up their title from their past life of hating cops. Now they were Christian and the street people could relate to them and their music.

The drummer and his wife sat down in the back of the room. When Mark greeted them, they made it clear that they didn't want anything to do with this 'Christian stuff.' They just came to hear the music. That's all. His wife carried *The Communist Manifesto*.

"That's okay," Mark said. "We're glad you came."

A few nights later, the front door burst open and the drummer dashed into the house. His eyes were dark and fearful.

"You need to tell me," he said, grabbing Mark. Out of breath, he could hardly speak.

"Tell you what?"

"Is this stuff true?"

"What stuff?"

"*The Exorcist.*"

"You mean the movie?"

"Yeah, I just saw it, man. It freaked me out."

"There's some truth to it," Mark said. "You just have to keep in mind that it was presented Hollywood style. But yes, I believe there are demonic forces in the world."

"Then I need help," he said. "Please, you need to help me." He clung to Mark.

"Okay," Mark said. "Just calm down. You'll be okay here. Just relax." He called over several members of 'The Happy Pigs' band that were at the house. "We need to pray for this man," Mark said.

The group gathered in a small circle around the young man and began to pray for him. When they finished, peace replaced the fear that had been on his face. What was now in his heart, shone through his eyes.

"Thank you," he said. "Thank you. I feel so good."

"That's God's peace you're feeling," Mark said. "It's better than any drug high you could ever get."

When everyone settled down for the night, Mark went upstairs to check on Becky and the new baby. They had named the child Sara. Mark felt so proud as he looked in on the baby sleeping quietly. Then he noticed that Becky wasn't there. Frantically Mark looked in the closet. When he found most of Becky's clothes were gone, Mark felt like someone had hit him in the stomach with a brick.

He went over to the bed and then slid to his knees.

"God, I don't understand this. All the miracles, the answers to prayer, why is this happening again?" He wept.

The next morning Mark was in the kitchen having a cup of coffee, trying to decide what to do about Becky. He hadn't slept all night. Dragging her home each time she took off didn't help.

Suddenly he heard shouting from upstairs. He walked to the bottom of the stairs and listened. It was Pam and Scotty. They were fighting again. They were married and Pam had come to the house for help because Scotty was physically abusing her. Mark was counseling with them, but Scotty didn't really want to change.

Mark ran up the stairs two steps at a time and knocked on their bedroom door. "Scotty, open this door right now!" Mark shouted.

The room grew quiet, except for Pam's soft crying.

"I said, open this door," Mark said, pounding on the door.

Scotty opened it. "Everything's okay," he said. "Don't worry about it."

"I can hear you yelling from downstairs and you're trying to tell me everything's okay? You better not have hit her."

Pam stood in the background holding her hand over her cheek.

"It doesn't matter what you think," he said to Mark. "I'm leaving." He turned and looked at Pam. "You coming?"

"No. I'm leaving. You need to stay and get help." She started to grab things in the room, tossing them into a suitcase.

"Come on, Pam," Scotty said, suddenly changing his tone of voice to kindness. "I don't want you to leave me."

"We can't live like this," she said, wiping tears from her face. "I can't take it anymore."

"Fine," he said. "You stay here. I'm leaving." He brushed past Mark, ran down the stairs and slammed the front door as he left.

Mark sighed. "Pam, I'm sorry."

"It's not your fault," she said. "He just doesn't want to deal with anything." She hesitated, then asked, "Is it okay if I stay for a while?"

"You stay as long as you want to," he said. "In fact, I really could use your help today. Can you take care of Sara?"

"Sure, I can. I just love her to pieces."

"Thanks," Mark said. "She'll probably be awake soon."

As he turned to walk down the hallway, Mark noticed that someone had taped a note on the outside of each door. He walked over to the first one, looked at it, then grinned.

"What is it?" Pam asked.

"A copy of the alphabet in sign language."

"Don." she said.

"Right. He thinks everyone in the house should learn sign language."

Mark headed downstairs and Don scurried over to him. He was holding a clipboard.

"What have you got there?" Mark asked.

Don scowled, then tapped his finger on the notepad. He handed it to Mark.

Mark read the first page, then flipped to the next. Don stood ramrod straight, military style, as if he were reporting in to his superior officer. Mark tried not to laugh as he read the scribbled pages.

"What are you, the Gestapo?" Mark finally asked. "What's this for? You've recorded everything anybody did wrong in the last few days."

Don nodded his head up and down and remained serious.

"Someone went out on the fire escape and had a cigarette in the middle of the night?" Mark read from one of the pages.

Don scowled and nodded as he acted out the motions of someone smoking a cigarette.

"Okay, Don. Good work. I'll take care of this. Anybody who breaks the rules has to answer to me."

Don gave one quick nod, then walked away with a satisfied smile. Mark laughed all the way to the kitchen. He poured himself another cup of coffee and began pondering how to explain Becky's absence. Maybe it was time to just tell everyone the whole story. He was tired of covering up.

The phone interrupted his thoughts.

"Anchor House, Mark speaking."

"Mark, my name is Jim Johnson and I'm calling for the local Jaycees. We could use your help with something."

"I'll help if I can," Mark said.

"We go into Chillicothe Correctional and work with some of the inmates there. What we really need is a class on drug and alcohol abuse. That's where you come in. We've heard about the good work you're doing at Anchor House and feel that you have an insight and perspective on this problem that the rest of us don't."

"I'd be glad to help." Mark said. "You set it up and I'll teach."

"Great. Would you be willing to do a class for the guards, too?"

Mark laughed. "Hey, if they can handle an ex-con telling them how to deal with inmates, I'll do it."

"Believe me, it won't be a problem. They're ready for some help. I'll get back to you. And thanks."

Mark went through his daily routine of counseling, leading a Bible study for those in the house and went out to speak to one of the local civic groups at a luncheon meeting. When he returned to the house, he checked the mail. One envelope stood out from the rest. It was bordered in black and addressed to Mark.

Pam came down the stairs, carrying the baby.

"Look, your daddy's home," she said.

Mark didn't respond to her. He tore open the envelope and read the card inside. Unspoken pain filled his eyes. He took a deep breath and felt as if his chest would burst.

Pam didn't know whether to say anything, so she stood there silently, holding the baby.

Mark carefully slipped the card back inside the torn envelope, hands trembling. He placed it on the table with the rest of the mail and his shoulders slumped in despair. He walked past Pam without even glancing at her. His chest heaved several times, but there were no tears. He went upstairs.

Pam walked over to the table and opened the envelope. It was from Nancy. She had a little girl after Mark left five years earlier. Her name was Evonne, and she had just died.

Pam heard Mark's sobs floating through the house. She sat in a rocking chair in the living room and clung to little Sara who was just an infant. She began rocking back and forth and her tears mingled with the sounds of Mark's anguish coming from upstairs.

Chapter Eleven

The house continued to bustle with activity. As a result of Mark teaching at the prison, he took in several inmates when they were released. He helped them find a job and get established on their own.

Pam became part of the staff, working with some of the women and doing most of the cooking. She also took care of little Sara much of the time. Becky came and went several times and Pam realized what was happening. She didn't say anything about it, not wanting to embarrass Mark. But she wondered how many people knew.

One day Mark got an invitation to speak in Florida at the Lakeland Jesus Festival. The people planning it wanted speakers that could relate to street people. They had a lot of bands coming in, too. Mark accepted.

While at the festival, he met some people involved with a ministry called The Jesus House. They invited Mark to join them at the house for a prayer meeting. Mark went, expecting something similar to what he was doing in Chillicothe. But when he entered the house, he knew their philosophy was different than his.

Filled with clutter, the house reminded Mark of one where a group of addicts would get together and crash. Although the youth staying at the house seemed to have really committed their lives to God, they hadn't dealt with their old habits. Mark believed in keeping a house clean and everyone being responsible for their own mess.

He spent some time talking and praying with them and when the meeting was over one of them said, "Mark, I believe God is telling me that you should move to Florida and take over this house."

Surprised, Mark looked at him, then looked around at the mess.

"Listen, brother, I appreciate that. But if the Lord has really told you that, then He can also tell me. Until He does, I plan to stay right where I am in Chillicothe."

Mark tried to dismiss the whole thing, but it ate away at him.

"Why in the world would I want to start all over again?" he mumbled to himself. "I've got a thriving ministry going. A good staff. A nice house. A clean house. And a great Board of Directors who are involved in the community. Why would I leave all that and go to Florida?"

Back in Ohio, he couldn't shake the thoughts. He began to feel like he was wrestling with God. He saw the potential of the ministry in Florida with the right kind of leadership, but he didn't want to go.

"I'm getting a regular paycheck here. Miracles are happening in people's lives. I'm well established. Why would I want to leave?"

Weeks went by and one morning when Mark sat reading his Bible, he clearly heard that still, small voice of God.

"Take a look at everything around you, Mark. I gave all this to you. You listened to My voice before. Why not now? If you're disobedient, just think of what you might be missing."

"God, are you trying to tell me that you could take all this away from me if I don't obey?"

Silence.

"But I don't like Florida. I don't like palmetto bugs. And I hate rattlesnakes."

Silence.

"I can't function in hot weather. And another thing. Southerners tend to be prejudiced. A dark-skinned Puerto

Rican like me wouldn't exactly be welcomed with open arms."

The still, small voice persisted.

Mark sighed. "Okay, if this is really what You want, Lord, then I'm laying out a fleece like Gideon did. And I'm not telling anyone what the fleece is."

Mark thought for a moment.

"Have the Board of Directors of that ministry call me from Florida and offer me $500 towards my moving expenses."

Mark smiled. He knew that amount of money would be hard for them to come up with. He saw how little they had.

His sense of relief over his "fleece" was short-lived. A few days later he received a phone call from Florida.

"Brother Mark, this is Pastor Johnson from Florida."

"Hello, Pastor Johnson. How are you?" Mark's heart beat a little faster. Wayne Johnson was on the Board of Directors down there.

"Mark, we were praying for you at our little meeting tonight and we feel we've heard a word from God..."

Mark closed his eyes.

"...We feel that God told us to call you and ask you again to move to Florida and take over this house ministry."

Mark didn't answer.

"We also felt led to collect some money for you right then and there at the meeting."

Mark sighed in relief. There's no way their small prayer group would come up with the amount of his 'fleece'.

"Praise God, we collected $500 to send to you."

"Five hundred?"

"Yes. We really feel God has spoken, Mark."

"Give me a little time and I'll get back to you."

"Okay, Mark. We'll be praying."

Mark hung up and stared at the phone.

"God, why do you want me to leave this place? Look how far I've come. From the filthy streets and basements of New York City...to this. Working with prominent people. Good people. I'm supposed to give all this up and move to an old house in the middle of the woods?"

Mark sat in silence for a long time.

Later that day, he called a staff meeting and told them what had happened. Becky was there, too. The staff didn't know how to react. They didn't want him to leave, but they didn't want to get in God's way either.

"If God speaks to any of you to come to Florida with me, you're welcome," Mark said. "I want you to be praying about it."

Becky wanted to go and once again, Mark hoped that a move to Florida might help their relationship. Maybe if she got completely away from any city life her problem would come under control.

Three of the staff decided to go. Pam, Betty and Lugene. And, of course, Don Butcher. He was excited about the move. This was a whole new experience for him after living in one location his entire life. He scurried around the house, helping everyone to pack. He couldn't wait to get on the road.

Chapter   Twelve

"This is going to take some adjusting," Mark said as he pulled the car up in front of the 100 year-old schoolhouse. It was the ministry house. "From the city, to this."

They all piled out of the two cars they had driven.

"This is definitely country living," Pam said.

"More like the boonies." Becky looked around at the lawn. The grass was pretty high. "Don't they own a lawnmower?"

"Come on, gang," Mark said, trying to be cheerful. "This is an adventure. Just think, this old schoolhouse is part of local history."

"Right. History," Becky mumbled.

"Just get a whiff of that air," Mark said, taking a deep breath.

"What is it?" Pam asked.

"Orange blossoms."

"Hey, we'll be able to pick our oranges right off the trees." Pam smiled.

"Now you're getting the spirit," Mark said.

The small group followed Mark into the house, stepping through the French double doors and into the living room.

"Look at that beautiful old fireplace." Mark walked over to it and ran his hand across the mantle. His hand was black with dust.

"Who needs a fireplace in Florida?" Becky said.

Mark turned and looked at her.

"Well, I suppose it would be nice on those few cool nights in the winter."

"Come look in here," Pam called from another room.

The group joined her.

"Look at this beautiful mural," she said. "Snow-capped mountains...in Florida."

Mark laughed. "To go with the fireplace."

They continued through the house, checking out the small kitchen with a picnic table in it, then the downstairs bedroom. They tramped up the curved wooden staircase to the second floor.

"Only two bedrooms up here," Pam said. "It's going to be a bit crowded."

"We'll manage," Mark said.

"How many are staying here right now?" Pam asked, looking around at the mess.

"I'm not sure. About five or six guys, I think. And don't worry about the mess. We'll be making some changes around here."

Later, when the men in the house returned from a trip into town, Mark gathered them and the staff together in the living room.

"The Bible says that unless the Lord builds a house, they that labor, labor in vain," Mark said. "I want to dedicate this house to the Lord. I know it needs some work and some cleaning up. But there's a lot of potential here. With God's help, we're going to provide a house that will be an anchor in the lives of those who come through these doors. And they'll know that they're loved."

The small group formed a circle and held hands while they bowed their heads in prayer.

Lying in bed that night, Mark said to Becky, "God reminded me today of a prayer meeting I attended a long time ago in Newark, Ohio. Joe Jordon was speaking. He was from Texas and had no idea who I was. I remember him pointing his finger at me and calling me to come up out of the audience."

" 'I don't know who you are,' he said, 'but I feel led to tell you something. God has shown me that you're going to be involved with helping kids some day. The people in the community will bring boys to you that need help and they will see through you, how great God is.' "

"Ummm...," Becky mumbled, falling asleep.

"Time to get up," Mark said cheerfully to one of the men sleeping at the house.

"What?" He groaned, squinting up at Mark. "What time is it?"

"It's seven o'clock."

"Seven in the morning? Are you crazy?" He rolled over and closed his eyes.

"Come on," Mark said. "Coffee is ready. It's time to get up. Then we need to discuss the rules of the house."

"Rules? What rules?" He opened his eyes and looked at Mark.

"Just get up and come downstairs. We'll talk about it." He glanced around at the others, all trying to ignore him and go back to sleep.

"All of you," Mark said. "Downstairs."

Slowly, everyone crawled out of bed and trailed downstairs to the living room. Mark posted a chart on the wall while they each grabbed a cup of coffee.

"This is our new schedule," he said, tapping the chart.

"Hey, man. Wait a minute. What's all this talk about a schedule?"

"Yeah," another said. "We don't need a schedule. We just do whatever the Lord leads us to do each day."

"Yes, I can see that," Mark said, glancing around the room. He smiled at them. "But now the Lord has led me here. And He's leading me to make some changes."

They all glared at him.

"Listen, I believe God wants us to be a good example to others; to have a clean house, a disciplined lifestyle. These are the kind of rules that will set you free. Free to fulfill God's plan for your life."

They all sat in silence, sipping on their coffee.

Mark ignored their icy stares and continued.

"We'll start every morning at seven o'clock. From seven until seven-thirty, you'll clean your room and get dressed. Breakfast will be served at seven-thirty, with everyone taking turns with the work schedule. Devotions will be at eight o'clock."

He looked around the room, from face to face. "Any questions so far?"

"I don't believe this," one of them groaned.

"There will be no more free lunches," Mark said. "Everyone here needs to pitch in and help with any work that needs to be done. You're going to get a job and learn to take on some responsibility."

"Job? Did you say job?"

"That's right," Mark said. "A real live job."

They ate breakfast in silence, then went upstairs to their bedroom. One by one, they came down with their few personal belongings packed.

"We're leaving," they said.

Pam was in the kitchen cleaning up after breakfast. She yelled to Mark in the living room. "I'm planning dinner for tonight. Will everyone be here?"

"I don't think so," Mark called back.

Pam came out, wiping her hands on a towel. "What happened?"

"They all left when I mentioned work. Especially when I mentioned 'job.' It looks like it will just be our own little group for dinner."

"Don't you worry," Pam said. "I have a feeling there are a lot of boys out there that we're going to be feeding."

Mark glanced around the large living room.

"We're going to fill this place up," he said. "No, God is going to fill this place up."

"We'll be bursting at the seams before you know it," Pam said, heading back to the kitchen.

Mark went outside and walked around the property.

"Okay, Lord, this is Yours. I know you brought me here for a reason. Here it is my first day. My plan was to get the house cleaned up. Instead, it got cleaned out." He walked over to one of the orange trees. "But, you know what? I'm not going to worry about it. I'll be faithful one day at a time. You can do the rest." He walked into the house, whistling.

Getting a cup of coffee, he went into the tiny office and sat down at the desk. Someone had already done a little cleaning in there.

"Probably Pam," he thought. "She's a good worker."

He began going through the ledgers and the checkbook left by the former director. His mood gradually changed as he checked everything thoroughly. Leaning back in his chair, he let out a long sigh.

"Lord, what am I going to do about this mess?"

"What's the matter with you?" Becky stood in the doorway.

"Bills. Nothing but bills," he said. "The mortgage on this place hasn't been paid in months. It looks like the bank is getting ready to foreclose." He held up one of the papers. "This is a warning that the electricity is about to be shut off if the bill isn't paid. I can't believe this place has survived as long as it has.

"Maybe it would survive a little longer if you wouldn't be so hard on people," she said.

"What are you talking about?"

"Your first morning and you post the rules on the wall. No wonder they all left."

"They left because they don't want to work."

She stood in the doorway and sighed.

"Becky, listen. I don't want to fight with you. You know what I believe. People have to learn to take on some responsibility so that they can eventually take care of themselves."

"Yeah, right. So what are you going to do about the bills?"

"I don't know." He got up from his desk. "I've got to get out and meet the people in the community and in the local churches. They need to know that we're here and what we plan to do. I'm sure some of them will help us."

Becky walked to the front door with him.

"One of the first things I'm going to do is change the name of the ministry to Anchor House." He gave Becky a hug and left.

When Mark returned at dinner time, everyone gathered for devotions.

"I really need your prayers," he said.

"You don't look like you had a great day," Betty said. "What happened?"

"Everywhere I went, I felt like I didn't fit in. Even with some of the Christians. Some of these Southerners are prejudiced. The whites looked at me like I was black. The blacks didn't fully accept me because I'm really not one of them, either. This dark Puerto Rican skin is not an asset down here."

"What makes you think it was up north?" Betty grinned at him.

Mark looked at her, then started laughing.

"Well, I guess God knows what He's doing," Mark said. "Just wait until the people who think I'm black, see Becky. A white, blonde wife. That will really shock them."

Everyone laughed. Everyone but Becky. She got up and left the room.

Chapter Thirteen

Pam had cleaned up after breakfast and came out into the living room. Little Sara broke into a grin and held out her arms when she saw Pam. She was just starting to speak a few words.

"Momma." she said.

Pam laughed and picked her up.

Becky shot up out of her chair and snatched Sara away from Pam.

"This is not your Momma," she scolded the baby. "I'm your Momma."

"Becky, I'm sorry, but she's just confused."

"It's your fault that she is," Becky snapped.

"Wait a minute, Becky." Pam took a deep breath, trying to control her anger. "It's time for me to say something to you. I'm the one around here doing the cooking and cleaning. I'm the one who takes care of Sara most of the time. Maybe if you started acting more like a mother, Sara wouldn't be so confused." Pam's face reddened and she stalked off to her room.

Mark came out of his office.

"What was that shouting all about?"

"Nothing, Mark." Becky looked at him and forced a smile. "It was nothing. Pam's just a little tired."

"She has been working hard."

"Betty and Lugene have been helping her. She'll be okay."

"I just got a call from a local newspaper reporter," he said. "They want to do a story on Anchor House. When they did the one in Chillicothe, it opened a lot of doors for us. Maybe this will be the same."

A few days after the article appeared, a taxi cab pulled up in front of Anchor House. An elderly man climbed out and marched to the front door.

"What can I do for you?" Pam asked.

He thrust the newspaper article in her face and thumped it with a bony finger.

"Is this article true?" he demanded.

"Yes."

"You take anybody in who needs help or a place to stay?"

"That's right."

"Good."

He turned and strutted back to the taxi cab, motioning for the driver to get out. After a brief exchange of comments and money, the driver popped open the trunk and took out several suitcases, carrying them up to the house.

"Thank you," the man said to the driver. Then he turned to Pam. "Now, where's my room?"

"Well, uh, if you'll just give me a few minutes, I'll have it ready for you," Pam said. "Then we need to talk."

"Fine."

"By the way, what's your name?"

"Charlie."

When Mark arrived home that afternoon, Pam said "Mark, I'd like you to meet Charlie."

Charlie slowly got out of his chair and stood erect.

"Hello, Charlie," Mark said, smiling.

"You the director here?" Charlie asked.

"That's right."

"Then you're the one I need to talk to."

"No problem," Mark said. "Why don't you stay for dinner? That will give us more time."

"Uh, Mark," Pam said. "He'll be here for many dinners."

"Oh?"

"Uh-huh. He moved in today."

"I see." Mark gave Pam a questioning look. "Well, welcome to Anchor House, Charlie."

Over dinner, Charlie explained that he had been living in an old hotel room in town. But the hotel was being renovated and he had to move out. He had no place to go, no family to turn to.

"Then I read the article in the newspaper about Anchor House," Charlie said. "I decided to come out and see if you people were 'for real'."

"And now what do you think?" Mark asked him.

"So far, so good," he said with a twinkle of mischief in his eyes.

Everyone laughed.

"I've been a Christian for many years," Charlie said. "And I just love kids. If you'll let me stay here, I'll help in any way that I can. I can do little things around the house."

"Welcome to our family," Mark said, extending his hand to Charlie.

"Thank you." his gray eyes glistened.

The phone rang and Mark went to his office to answer it.

"Anchor House."

"Mark, this is Tim. I don't know if you remember me. You spoke at our church this week and we talked for a while afterwards."

"Yes, Tim, I remember you. You work with HRS, right?"

"Yes, and I have a favor to ask."

"What is it?"

"I have a boy who's been in and out of several juvenile institutions and programs. He gets in one place, stirs up trouble, then gets placed in another program. No one seems to be able to get through to him. Are you willing to give it a try?"

"Sure. Has he had much one-on-one counseling? Or has

he just been pushed through programs?"

"He'd had all kinds of professional counseling. But it hasn't made one bit of difference in his behavior."

"I'm curious," Mark said. "Why did you call me?"

"I know from what you've said that you'll love him and that you'll tell him about Jesus."

"That I can guarantee," Mark answered.

"There's one more thing you should know."

"What's that?"

"He's Jewish."

"One of God's chosen," Mark said. "Bring him over and we'll talk. If he's open to staying here with us, I'd be glad to take him in."

Tim arrived the next morning with Robin.

Robin was tall, lean, and had shoulder-length sandy hair. He wore a tattered t-shirt and his thin legs protruded from a pair of baggy, ragged shorts. The set of his chin suggested a stubborn streak.

"Welcome to Anchor House," Mark said.

Robin glanced around the room, noticing all the Christian posters.

"Let's get something straight," he said to Mark. "I'm a Jew and plan to remain a Jew. I have no interest in what you 'Jesus freaks' have to say."

"Son, I didn't ask if you believed in Jesus. Or even if you believed in God. But I'm glad to hear that you're a Jew."

Robin looked at Mark with skepticism.

"I am," Mark said. "I thank the Jews for Jesus Christ."

"Right."

"Listen Robin, all I know is that HRS needs a place for you and you're welcome to stay here."

"Yeah? So where's my room?" He plopped himself in a living room chair.

Mark glanced at Tim.

"Well, I have to get going, Mark. I sure do appreciate your willingness to help us out." He shook Mark's hand and quickly left.

"Come on in my office, Robin. Let's have a little talk."

"Here comes the lecture," Robin mumbled under his breath.

When they were both seated, Mark said "Let's go over the rules of the house."

Robin groaned and slouched down in his chair.

"Every morning when you get up, you clean up your room. If you need to go somewhere or make a phone call, you have to ask permission. We'll feed you well, but if you want a snack in between meals, you need to ask. You can't just raid the refrigerator."

Robin glared at him and didn't respond.

"In this house you can get just about anything you want, if your attitude is right. The rules are only to help you develop some good habits. There's a chart on the wall with our daily schedule, so there's no need to review that right now. You can read it yourself. Any questions?"

"Nope." He remained slouched in his chair, arms crossed.

"Robin, listen to me. I will not compromise my faith for anyone. But neither will I ever force it on anyone."

"First good news I've heard."

Mark stood and extended his hand towards Robin. "I'm glad you're here, Robin. Welcome to Anchor House."

"Yeah, so when do we eat?" Robin asked.

Mark laughed. "Come on," he said. "Let's raid the refrigerator together."

The first few days Robin cooperated with the schedule, but wouldn't communicate with anyone. He only spoke when necessary. The third day, he disappeared. Mark called Tim and reported him missing.

A few days later, Tim called back.

"We found Robin," he said. "He got busted with his girlfriend in Daytona. He's being held in the Detention Center."

"I'll send someone to pick him up," Mark said. "It is okay if he comes back here, isn't it?"

"Sure, if you still want him."

"Of course, I do. The kid has a lot of potential. He just needs someone to stand by him through all of this."

The next day Robin stepped into Mark's office and plunked himself down in a chair. Mark ignored him for a few minutes and completed some paperwork.

Finally, he looked up, leaned back in his chair, and just looked at Robin. He didn't speak.

Robin sat with his arms folded tight across his chest, staring at his feet. Feeling awkward in the silence, he finally looked at Mark and spoke.

"Why did you send someone to get me?"

"Because I care about you. That's why."

"But why?"

"Why do I care about you?"

"Yeah. Why should you? Nobody else does." Uncomfortable, Robin shifted his eyes to his feet again.

"Because I know what it feels like to be your age and feel totally rejected. I lived on the streets of New York City and had to fight to survive. Sometime soon I'll share the whole story with you. Right now, you need to take a shower and get settled back in your room."

Robin got up and started to leave the office.

"Wait a minute," Mark said, coming out from behind his desk. "I want you to know that I really do care about you." He put his arm around Robin's shoulders. "And whether you believe it or not, God does too."

Robin cleared his throat as if to say something, but didn't.

His attitude changed day by day, responding to the love he felt in the house. Those at HRS and others that had known Robin were amazed at the change.

Within a short time calls began coming in asking for help with other boys in trouble. Mark continued to go out and speak at the schools, churches and civic groups. The house soon bulged at the seams with 20 boys, plus staff.

Chapter Fourteen

"Where's Becky?" Mark asked Betty, one of the staff.

"I don't know. She left about an hour ago, but didn't say where she was going."

Mark went to their bedroom. Becky had been very moody for some time and often contradicted Mark in front of the boys. A real coolness had developed in their relationship.

In the bedroom, he glanced on the dresser to see if she might have left a note about where she was going. There was none. Then he noticed a letter lying there. He picked up the envelope beneath it. The return address was Chillicothe and it was addressed to Becky.

Mark stood there for a moment, looking at the letter. His gut feeling told him something was wrong. He unfolded the letter and began to read. It was from Becky's lover. Mark felt nauseous. Then angry. He sat down on the edge of the bed and read the letter again.

The bedroom door swung open. It was Becky.

"What's this?" Mark shouted, holding up the letter.

"It's nothing," Becky said, snatching the letter from his hands. "What are you doing opening my mail?"

"Opening your mail? It was already opened. Lying right out on the dresser. I didn't have to open it."

"It's none of your business," she screamed.

"None of my business?!" Mark paced back and forth. "Right. It's none of my business. It's none of my business that my wife lies to me! It's none of my business where you go, or what you do, or who you see!" He grabbed the letter out of her hand, crumpled it and tossed it across the room.

"Calm down," she said sarcastically. "You might ruin your image with the boys."

"I'm sick and tired of your lies," Mark continued. "And I'm fed up with your rotten attitude around here. I don't have to put up with this. It's over between us."

"That's fine with me," she fumed. "I was planning to leave anyway." She pulled a suitcase out of the closet and began stuffing her things into it.

"If you leave again, don't plan to come back," Mark threatened. "This time it will mean divorce."

"Do whatever you want." She snapped the suitcase shut and stormed out of the room, slamming the door behind her.

Mark fell to his knees next to the bed and his whole body shook with sobs.

The next day he went and talked to a pastor, explaining what had happened over the last few years.

"It sounds to me like you never really had a marriage, Mark. And you certainly have grounds for a divorce."

"But I don't know how it would affect the ministry," Mark said. "I don't want to do anything that will hurt these boys."

"If your personal life is in constant turmoil it will eventually affect the ministry anyway. You need to take care of this issue once and for all."

Several months later, Mark and Becky were divorced. She kept Sara with her.

Chapter Fifteen

One morning during prayer time with the boys, Mark told them to pray specifically for enough money to come in that week to cover their mortgage payment.

"As you boys know, we depend on donations to keep this house open," he said. "With so many of you here, our bills have increased and our finances are very tight right now."

"If we don't get the money, does that mean we won't be able to stay here anymore?" The boy who asked the question sounded fearful.

"No," Mark said. "God will take care of our needs. I don't want you to be worrying about it. I just want you to join with me and pray about it." He looked around the room at the boys' faces. He grinned at them. "Then we'll watch God do His thing."

A few boys grinned back at him. Some looked skeptical. But they all prayed.

The next day a woman came to the Anchor House and asked to speak with Mark. She was the mother of one of the boys who had stayed at Anchor House for a while.

"Mark, you were so good to my son when he needed help. He's really changed. At the time, I had no money to give to you, but now I do."

She handed him a check.

"Please accept this as part of my thanks for everything you've done."

"Praise God," Mark said.

After she left, he called all the boys into the living room.

"Do you remember our prayer yesterday morning?"

They nodded.

"I'm going to pass this check around the room and I want you to take a good look at it. This is God's answer to our prayer. It will cover our mortgage payment."

"Wow, that's great," one of them said.

"I didn't think we'd get it."

"I did," another said. "God's pretty smart, you know."

Mark laughed and the others joined him.

"Okay, enough celebrating," Mark said. "Back to your chores and your homework."

Mark went into his office to make a phone call to a friend in the HRS office. He was concerned about one of the boys he had just taken in.

"I need you to check out this kid's background," Mark said. "I think he has some very serious mental problems."

"Sure, I'll check him out."

A few days later, his friend called back.

"Mark, you have a pretty dangerous situation there. That boy doesn't belong in your house. He needs psychiatric care. Looking over his file, I see a lot of violence and think he needs to be isolated for the safety of those around him."

"I knew it," Mark said. "There's just something about him. I really would like to work with him, but I can't sacrifice the safety of the other boys."

"Listen, let's make a deal," his friend said.

"Why does that make me nervous?" Mark asked.

"Hey, we're friends, right? Would a friend give you a bad deal?"

"Okay, okay. What's the deal?"

"We have someone else here who needs a place to stay. He's a little older and has had some problems, but nothing really serious. Let me bring him over to stay with you, and I'll take the problem kid off your hands. This guy can work around the house and the yard. He'll earn his room and board.

How about it?"

"Don Butcher helps keep up with the yard work," Mark said. "But sure, why not. Bring him over."

Jack didn't communicate much when he first arrived at Anchor House. He obeyed the rules and did his share of the work, but pretty much stayed by himself. Mark didn't pressure him and very gradually, Jack began opening up.

"Can I talk to you about something?" he asked Mark one day.

"Of course. Let's go to my office."

Jack sat in a chair, fidgeting with his hands.

"What is it?"

Jack cleared his throat. "Well, I really appreciate you letting me stay here and I don't mind working around the house but I feel like I should be out working and earning some money."

"If you're ready to get a job, that's great," Mark said.

"You don't mind?"

"Of course not. Why would you think I'd have a problem with you getting a job?"

"Uh..."

The phone rang, interrupting their conversation. Mark answered it and asked the caller to wait a moment. Covering the mouthpiece, he asked Jack, "Was there anything else we need to discuss?"

Jack hesitated. "No," he said, standing up. He started to leave the office.

"Jack," Mark called after him. "Do you have a job lined up already?"

Jack swung around and looked at Mark, hesitating. "Yes, I think so."

"Good," Mark said. "We'll talk again later."

A few days later Mark tapped on Jack's bedroom door, then stepped into the room.

"Jack, are you getting ready for work?"

Standing in front of his dresser, Jack swung around and his face paled. He didn't answer.

"What are you so nervous about?"

He stood, frozen.

Mark glanced around the room. On the bed, a woman's dress was laid out. He walked over to the dresser where Jack stood. Jack stepped aside.

"What's this?" Mark asked, picking up a box filled with makeup. "What's going on here?"

Jack started shaking and didn't answer.

"I said, what's going on here?" Mark spoke in a low, but firm tone of voice.

"I...I'm a female impersonator," Jack stuttered.

Mark searched Jack's face. Putting his hands on his shoulders, he forced him against the bedroom wall.

"I don't see a girl in those eyes," Mark said. "I see a man."

Jack's body trembled. Tears streamed down his face.

"You don't have to live like this," Mark said. "God created you to be a man. If you go against that, you're headed for some pretty serious problems."

Jack put his hands over his face and began sobbing. Mark let him cry for a few minutes, then took him into his office to talk. Afterwards, Jack agreed to quit his job as a female impersonator and over the next few months Mark saw a gradual change take place in him. He began to develop more masculine traits. After several more months, Jack left the Anchor House to join the Army.

"You're going to be okay," Mark said.

"I know," Jack said. "I feel good about myself now."

Chapter Sixteen

Mark gathered all the boys in the living room after dinner one evening. Some sat on the sofa and chairs, some sprawled out on the floor.

"We have a problem," he began. "There are 25 of you living here right now. You all like to eat, right?"

They nodded in agreement.

"You also like to take showers."

"Some of us do, some of us don't," one boy said, snickering.

"Well, this is your house," Mark continued, "and when there's a problem, it's your problem too. Right now we need a supply of soap. Soap for dishes, washing clothes, and for cleaning up a few bodies around here."

"So you want us to pray about it?"

"That's right. God can supply all our needs. But He expects us to ask."

"We're going to ask God for soap?" the new boy asked.

"Yeah," someone answered. "You ain't seen nothin' yet. Pop prays for everything."

"Go ahead," Mark said. "Make fun of me all you want. But God will have the last laugh. He always does."

He bowed his head and began to pray. The boys quieted down.

"God, show these boys just how real you are. I thank You that You care about our everyday needs. We need soap. I know that somehow you will supply it for us. Thank You. In Jesus' name, Amen."

The boys slowly got up and left the room.

"Is he for real?" the new boy asked, glancing towards Mark.

"Yeah, he's for real."

"This sure is different from Detention Center."

The next afternoon after the boys came home from school, Mark went outside to play a game of basketball with them. During the game, a pick-up truck pulled into the driveway.

A woman stepped out and shouted, "Is Mark Rivera here?"

"That's me," Mark said, walking towards the truck.

"I've got something for you," she said.

"Really? What?"

"In the back of the truck," she pointed. "Soap. All different kinds of soap, detergent and bleach."

"Hold on a minute," Mark said. He turned toward the boys still playing basketball.

"Hey, boys. Come over here a minute."

When they gathered around the truck, Mark asked the woman to repeat what she had just said to him.

"I've got cases of soap, detergent and bleach for you," she said.

"Wow! You really got soap?"

"Yes," she said, wondering what the big deal was.

"Just for the sake of these boys," Mark said, "did anyone tell you that we needed this stuff?"

"No. Several of us in the community know the work you're doing out here and wondered how we could help. I was driving by the Purex Company with a friend the other day and got the idea of asking them for these supplies for Anchor House. The management agreed and here I am."

"See, boys? See how God answers prayer?"

The new boy stood wide-eyed, staring into the back of the truck. "I don't believe this," he said.

"Okay," Mark said, clapping his hands together, "Let's unload this truck."

Several months later, a heavy rain storm left the yard flooded. The next day, the water still hadn't drained. Concerned, Mark called the county engineers to come out and check the yard.

"How many people live in this house?" the inspector asked Mark.

"There are 27 of us right now," Mark said.

"Twenty-seven?"

"Yes. We're a little cramped, but we manage."

"This house wasn't built to handle that many people," he said. "It could be that you're having a septic problem."

The next day another inspector came out, this time from the health department.

"I understand you have 27 people living in the house," he said.

"Yes, that's right," Mark answered.

"Don't you realize that the septic tank here was meant for a single family? There's no way it can handle the capacity you need."

"What can we do?"

"You need a new septic tank and drainage field."

Mark sighed. "We don't have money for that."

"Well, that's not our problem. It's something you're going to have to take care of. I wouldn't like to have to close this place down."

"Close us down?"

"You have to meet county specifications," he said. "I didn't make the rules. But I do have to enforce them. I'll get the paperwork together so you'll know exactly what's required."

"Okay," Mark said. "I know you're just doing your job."

"I need to check inside the house now," he said.

"I'll give you the grand tour."

Mark showed him through the downstairs first.

"Two staff members use this small back porch as a bedroom," he said. "I have my own room, and Charlie turns the dining room into a bedroom at night."

Upstairs, old army cots filled the two bedrooms.

"This is where the boys sleep," Mark said.

The inspector shook his head. "I have to add something else to my list."

"What's that?"

"You have to install another bathroom."

Pam came up the stairs, carrying cleaning supplies. Mark introduced her to the inspector.

"Where do you sleep?" he asked. "In the living room?"

"No, I moved out some time ago and room with another family. They're on our Board of Directors. We had another female on staff, but she got married and left." She looked at Mark. "What's this all about?"

"We have to install another bathroom."

"I'm sorry," the inspector said, "but I don't have any choice about this. And neither do you."

He left and Mark went into his office. He just sat, staring into space.

After a few minutes, Pam stuck her head in the doorway.

"Cheer up," she said. "God has done pretty good by us so far. Don't you think He'll continue?"

"Another bathroom...a new septic tank...a drainage field ..." Mark's voice drifted off.

"What you need to do is get out of here for a little while. A change of scenery will do you good."

Mark looked at her. "On one condition," he said.

"What's that?"

"You come with me. Otherwise, who can I complain to?" He smiled at her.

"I'll come on one condition."

"What's that?"

"This won't be a gripe session. That's the last thing either one of us needs right now."

"You're right. It's a deal. Come on, I'll buy you a cup of coffee somewhere."

"A cup of coffee? What a treat."

"Hey, no gripe session, remember? Besides, it's all I can afford. From now on, any extra money goes into the toilet."

Pam looked at him, then burst out laughing.

"What's wrong?" Mark asked Pam when he came back from speaking at a luncheon the next day. "You look as if you've lost your best friend."

"It's Charlie. I had to take him to the hospital."

"What happened?"

"He fell down the stairs and broke his hip. The doctor said that it will take a long time to heal, at his age. He feels that Charlie needs to be in a nursing home."

"We need to do whatever is best for him."

"I know. I just feel bad for him."

"So do I. We'll just have to make a point of visiting him regularly. How did things go with the boys this morning? "

"When they went off to school, they were worried," Pam said. "One of them told me that he didn't know what he'd do if Anchor House was closed down. He had no other place to go."

"We need to keep praying for a miracle," Mark said. "I was reading Matthew 19 this morning, where Jesus said, 'Suffer the little children to come unto Me, and forbid them not; for of such is the kingdom of heaven.' God will get us through this new crisis with the septic tank somehow."

A few weeks later, Mark was in his office when he heard the boys shouting outside. He went out to see what the commotion was all about.

"It's a giant bathtub!" one of the boys shouted.

"No, it's Noah's Ark."

They were laughing and pointing towards the street.

"What in the world," Mark said, watching the heavy equipment derrick pulling into the yard.

The driver stepped out.

"Mark Rivera?"

"That's me."

"A friend of yours from the Rotary Club sent this over for you."

"What is it," one of the boys asked, "a swimming pool?"

"No," the driver said, laughing. "I don't think you'll be swimming in this thing. It's a septic tank."

Mark just stood there, staring at it.

"God delivered us a septic tank?" one of the boys asked. "This is wild."

Everyone started laughing.

The driver explained that a local businessman bought two septic tanks for a building project he was working on, but then realized he only needed one. He decided to donate the second one to Anchor House.

Within a few weeks the new tank and drainage field were in place, as well as the new bathroom. People in the community heard about the need and enough donations came in to cover the costs.

Then the fire inspector showed up.

"Can't allow this," he said, walking around the outside of the house.

"What's wrong?" Mark asked.

"A fire escape. You need a fire escape for the second floor."

"A fire escape," Mark looked up at the sky. "We need a fire escape."

"I'd hate to see this place shut down," the inspector said.

"Don't worry," Mark said, "it won't be shut down."

"We've had some complaints."

"What kind of complaints?"

"Some people think you've got too many boys in here."

Mark gritted his teeth. "All I'm trying to do out here is help these kids. If someone doesn't step in and help them at this point in their lives, most of them will end up in jail and prison. They need to know that someone cares." His voice was full of frustration.

"I realize that. But when we get complaints, we need to follow up on them. Let's go inside. I need to check out the interior."

Mark tried to conceal his annoyance. "Follow me," he said.

As they walked through the house, the inspector said, "You need to install a sprinkler system in the ceilings."

"A sprinkler system? But we have fire extinguishers."

"Need those too. You need both. You won't pass inspection without a fire escape and a sprinkler system." He handed Mark a copy of his report and left.

Once again, Mark called the boys together for a special prayer time, explaining about the fire escape.

"Man, I thought prayer meetings would be a drag when I first got here," one boy said. "But I wouldn't miss this for anything. I wonder how God's going to deliver a fire escape?"

Everyone laughed, then settled down to pray.

A few weeks later, Mark received a phone call from a friend. "You're not going to believe this," he said. "I was driving up the highway today and glanced over to my right. There it was out in a field, just rusting."

"What?"

"Your fire escape!"

"My fire escape?"

"Yes." He chuckled. "I saw this fire escape laying out in a field. So I pulled off the road and asked several people if they knew who owned that property. I went and talked to the guy and he said he'd be glad to get rid of the thing. He said it needs a little welding, but other than that, it's in pretty good shape. His exact words to me were, 'If you come and get this sucker off my property, you can have it.'"

Mark started laughing.

"Isn't that great?"

"It sure is," Mark said. "It's wild. I can't wait to tell the boys."

Chapter Seventeen

One night Mark received a call from a leader in one of the local churches.

"Mark, our church group went out on the streets tonight, just to share with the kids who hang out."

"That's great, " Mark said.

"We picked up this one boy who has no place to stay. Can we bring him over?"

"Sure," Mark said. "We can always make room for one more."

In a short while they arrived. The boy was filthy and the stench of his clothes filled Mark's office.

"What's your name?"

"Jock."

"Well, Jock, let's get you cleaned up and fed," Mark said. "Then we'll talk in the morning."

Early the next morning, Mark's prayer time was interrupted by someone pounding on the front door.

"Open up this damn door!"

Mark hurried to the door and unlocked it.

"Are you the head of this place?" A large man stood there, eyes blazing.

"Yes, my name is Mark. What can I do for you?"

The man drew himself up to his full 6'2" height and pushed his way past Mark into the house with a rude determination.

"You take a new kid in last night?" He scowled at Mark.

"Yes," Mark said, keeping his voice low and calm.

"Well, you s.o.b., that's my kid. Now where is he?" He stood with his hands holding the straps of his bib overalls. A few days growth of beard stippled his face, his shirt was torn, and his shoes were covered with mud.

"He's eating breakfast. Now, why don't you just calm down. I'll get you a cup of coffee and we can talk."

"Talk?! Listen you..." His voice was deep and gruff. "I know what you got here. It's a cult. Another Jim Jones. And you damn well better get my boy out here right now."

Some of the boys in the house came into the living room when they heard all the shouting and cursing. Mark glanced over at them. They gave Mark the kind of look that said they were ready to jump in and fight this guy. All Mark had to do was give the word.

"It's okay, boys," Mark said, holding up his hand. "Just go back to your breakfast. But tell Jock to come out here. His father wants to see him."

Jock came out, obviously embarrassed.

"Hi ya, Pa," he said, trying to sound bright.

"What the hell you doin' here, boy?" his father demanded. "Don't you know better than to get messed up with a bunch of idiots like this?"

"All I did was spend the night. I'm ready to go now."

"You bet you are," he said, pushing his son out the front door. Then he turned and said to Mark, "You're a no good bum. I ought to call the police on you. Who knows what goes on out here."

"There's a phone in my office," Mark said, beginning to fume. "I'd be glad to let you use it."

"Why you ..." The man took a step towards Mark.

Mark held his hand up to stop him. "Let me tell you something. Your son ran away from home. I didn't go looking for him and drag him in here. And he probably left because of your rotten attitude—judging from what I see."

The man's eyes sparked with anger. As he started

towards Mark, a woman came screaming through the front door.

"What did you do to my boy? You think you can just snatch kids from their homes and drag them out here to be part of your cult?" She lunged at Mark, arms flailing. The man grabbed her.

"I'll take care of this, Lila. Get yourself back in the truck." He shoved her back out the front door and turned to Mark.

The man's face twisted into a threat. "You haven't heard the last of us, nigger." He spun around and marched out.

The boys had drifted back into the living room and stood in silence.

"We need to pray for Jock," Mark said. "At this point, that's all we can do for him."

After the boys went off to school for the day, Mark gathered the small staff for a meeting.

"That incident with Jock's parents hit the boys hard this morning," Don said.

"Do you know why?" Mark asked. "Most of them can relate to a scene like that. It's the kind of home many of them came from.

"Look at Charles. Ten years old. His father is an alcoholic, his mother is dead. He's been beaten and has cigarette burns all over his body from his drunken father.

"Michael—only twelve years old and sexually abused by his alcoholic mother.

"And then there's William. Eight years old and awaiting trial for murder. The newspapers called him a 'baby killer.' My God, he's just a baby himself. He was just fighting with a friend. The friend fell into a pond and drowned and now William is a 'killer.'

"Joey's mother called me and said, 'You've got to get my kid out of this house. He's on drugs. He doesn't go to school. Sometimes he beats me up. His stepfather is ready to kill him.' I remember the first day Joey came. He spit in my face when I read him the rules. But look at him now. He's changing. He feels accepted, loved. He's getting some self-esteem.

Then there's Billy. Eleven years old, found living in a Goodwill box, sleeping on some old rugs—abandoned. "

Mark's voice broke.

"What I'm trying to say is that what we're doing here is important. Whether people out there realize it or not; we're literally saving lives. And I want each of you to know just how much I appreciate your help. For sticking by me when things are tough and finances are limited. I love each one of you."

The small group spontaneously gathered around Mark and hugged him.

"We love you, too, Mark."

"And we'll keep on standing by you," Pam said.

They prayed for Mark, asked God to give him a renewed strength to continue with the work. Then, one by one, they each poured out their hearts before God, praying for each boy that was living in the house.

The phone was ringing when they finished and Mark answered it in his office.

"Listen, you white nigger, get ready, cause I'm goin' to blow your slimey Spic head off." A muffled, female voice snarled into the phone.

"Who is this?"

"Never you mind who this is. You're nothin' but a kinky-headed refugee and I'm on my way over to take care of you."

"Okay, Ma'am, I tell you what. I'll be outside waiting for you. If you really want to shoot me, it'll be easy. Come on over."

The phone slammed in Mark's ear.

Mark marched out of his office and headed for the front door, steaming.

"What's wrong?" Pam asked. "You look like you're ready to kill somebody."

"You've got it backwards. Actually, someone is ready to kill me. And I intend to face them head on." He turned towards the door.

"Wait a minute, Mark. What's this all about?"

Mark let out a long, slow breath, then told her about the phone call.

"Do you think it's that woman who was here this morning?"

"I don't know. It doesn't really matter. Nobody is going to intimidate me like that. Christians don't have to be wimps. I'll be outside."

He picked up a basketball and stomped out into the yard. He shot baskets for an hour; then for two hours. Finally, he went back inside. His anger had subsided.

"Apparently it was just a bluff," he said.

"Thank God," Pam whispered.

Mark slipped into bed that night worn out from the strain of the day.

Chapter Eighteen

One morning Mark called Pam into his office.

"Pam, it's been a while since Becky and I were divorced and I want you to know how much I have appreciated your support through all of this. You've gone through some tough and awkward situations with me."

"I know I'm right where God wants me," Pam said.

"I'd like to spend a little more time with you," Mark said. "We already have a good friendship and I...well, I know you're the kind of woman who would make a good wife to someone in ministry."

Pam's face reddened.

"I didn't mean to embarrass you," Mark said.

"No, it's okay. I just...I just wasn't expecting this."

"If you'd rather not..."

"No...I mean, yes. I'd like to spend more time with you, too."

Their eyes met for a moment, then they both laughed, breaking the awkwardness of the conversation.

"Okay. You've got a date for lunch," Mark said.

After several months of dating, Mark asked Pam to marry him.

"Mark, I've been praying about our relationship, too. There's just one problem."

"If you're having second thoughts...?"

"No, it's not that. I just think that we'll need some privacy in order for our marriage to work. I'm not sure we should live in the house with the boys. Until I moved out of here and in with Mary and Gene Cox, I didn't realize how important it is to have some time away from the kids at night. It prevents burn-out."

"I know it's hard to live where you work," Mark said. "But we don't have the finances to live anywhere else."

"Let's pray about it," Pam said. "Maybe something will open up."

"With me making $75 and you $25, that will be a real miracle," Mark said. "But we've seen plenty of those around here."

The following day Mark and Pam announced to everyone their plan to be married.

"Congratulations!" said Bobby, one of the newest staff members, as he gave them each a big hug. Then he said, "Hey, I've got a great idea."

"What's that?" Mark asked.

"My little house trailer is less than a mile from here. Why don't you and Pam move into my trailer and I'll room here at the Anchor House. That will give you some time to yourselves."

Pam looked at Mark, smiling.

"Thanks, Bobby," Mark said. "You don't know how much we appreciate that. It's a real answer to prayer."

"I've got another surprise for you," Mark said to Pam. "We're going on a honeymoon to Rome."

"Rome?!"

"Yes," Mark said with a mischievous grin. "Rome, Georgia."

The wedding took place at the Anchor House with The Reverend Gene Cox performing the ceremony. Pastor Wayne Johnson's wife planned the reception and arranged for flowers. Annette, who had been helping out with secretarial duties, made Pam's floor-length yellow wedding dress. Another friend made a three-tier wedding cake.

The entire Board of Directors, the boys in the house, local friends and pastors, came to celebrate with Mark and Pam.

After the ceremony, as Mark and Pam prepared to leave for their honeymoon in a borrowed car, their friend Tom handed Mark a set of keys to his little red Colt.

"I feel the Lord has told me to give this car to you," he said, handing Mark the keys. "It's yours. Not just to borrow for your honeymoon, but to keep. God bless you both."

When Mark and Pam pulled into the driveway, just returning from their honeymoon, they saw Todd sitting up in a tree in the yard, reading his Bible.

"Look at that," Mark said. "Can you believe he's reading his Bible?"

"I remember the day he called us from a phone booth, asking if he could come and live at Anchor House. I'll never forget when he walked in the door. A real hippie with long, stringy blonde hair and those low slung, dirty jeans. I was always telling him to pull them up."

"Remember how he squawked when I told him he had to work? He thought he was going to die." Mark chuckled. He parked the car and shut off the engine. "Now look at him. Reading his Bible. He came stoned on pot and didn't want anything to do with God. He sure has changed."

"It's the Todds that make it all worth it," Pam said.

"Did I tell you what he told me before we left on our honeymoon?" Mark asked.

Pam shook her head no.

"He said that God showed him Gloria was going to be his wife some day."

"Are you serious? She's not remotely interested in him. She comes to sing and play guitar for some of our meetings, but I know she's not interested in getting involved with any of the guys here."

"I know," Mark said. "I told him that if it was really God speaking to him, then it would just happen. Not to force it. He's only eighteen years old, but not a typical eighteen-year-old with all he's been through. We'll just have to keep an eye on the situation."

"A little romance at the Anchor House," Pam said, grinning.

They went inside to check in with the staff and see how things went while they were gone.

"I just got a call to see if we could take in a kid who got caught stealing a car last night," Paul said. "The police had quite a chase scene trying to catch him. They raced through the orange groves, dodging trees—the kid was driving a Cadillac with the lights turned off. Trouble is, we're really full up right now."

"How old is he?" Mark asked.

"Ten."

"Ten years old? And he stole a Cadillac?"

"Uh-huh. He could barely reach the pedals, but he did it. He must be a whiz of a driver to give the police a chase like that." He couldn't help but laugh.

Pam looked at Mark. "We could take him," she said.

"You mean to the trailer with us?"

"He's only ten, Mark. I'd feel bad if we didn't take him in."

He put his arm around her. "Me too," he said. "I just want to be sure you're comfortable with it."

"Let's do it."

"There goes our privacy."

She shrugged her shoulders. "This is more important."

Jimmy arrived the next day and moved in with Mark and Pam. He sat in a chair, grinning and swinging his legs back and forth while Pam told him the rules of the house. His feet didn't reach the floor. Pam wondered how he could ever drive a car. He was so short.

"Well, at least I don't have to worry about you taking my car," she said to him, teasing. "It's a stick shift."

"Hey, stick shifts are easy," he said. "All you do is push in the clutch, turn the key and start the engine, push on the gas just a little bit..." He went through the motions as he spoke.

"Don't even think about it," Pam warned.

"Okay," he said, still grinning from ear to ear.

The next day he disappeared for a few hours and Pam got worried. He was supposed to be playing with another boy in the neighborhood. But when she called the other boy's mother to check on him, they were both gone somewhere. She called Mark at his office.

"Is your car still there?" Mark asked.

"Yes, it's the first thing I checked," she said.

"I'll be right there. We'll have to go looking for him."

After she hung up with Mark, Pam got a phone call from the other boy's mother. Her son had returned, filthy dirty and said that Jimmy was still over in the phosphate pits driving around the big crane.

Mark came in as Pam hung up.

"Guess where he is," she said. "Over in the phosphate pits driving around the heavy construction equipment, a crane."

They walked through the woods to the phosphate mining field and sure enough, there he was. He was grinning from ear to ear as he drove the huge crane around in circles.

A few weeks later, Jimmy went back to his parents and they moved to Indiana.

A local judge called Mark one day and asked him if there was a spot available at the Anchor House for another boy.

"I have an eight-year-old," the judge said. "I think you're probably the only hope for him."

"What's he done?" Mark asked.

"He's been in court several times already for setting three different apartments on fire, shooting and killing a dog, and a few other miscellaneous things."

"Sounds like a challenge to me," Mark said. "Bring him over and I'll work with him."

"I need to warn you," the judge said, "he's got a real foul mouth."

"Believe me, he won't be the first one we've taken in with that problem."

Willy arrived that afternoon and Mark had Paul show him around the house and explained the rules. Willy did nothing but swear and complain. That night Mark got a phone call at the trailer.

"Mark, this is Paul. We're having trouble with this new kid."

"Willy?"

"Yes. He refuses to take a bath. He won't go to bed. He keeps picking fights with the older boys."

"Whoaa...slow down, Paul. All this from a little eight-year-old?"

"I'm telling you, this kid is a real problem. Even the older guys don't want to be anywhere near him. And some of these older kids have done things like armed robberies, but they're afraid of Willy. It's incredible."

"Why are they afraid of him? He's so little."

"They say he's like someone from *The Exorcist*."

Mark sighed. "Okay, I'll come over and talk to him."

"Now?"

"Yes. Now."

"Good. See you in a few minutes."

Mark went to the house and confronted Willy.

"I want you to get into the tub right now and take a bath. Then you're going to bed."

Willy glared at him. "You dirty s.o.b., I don't have to do what you tell me."

"Listen, Willy, Jesus loves you," Mark said in a soft voice.

Willy jammed his fingers in his ears and started shouting every cuss word he could think of.

Mark prayed, "I take authority over anything controlling this boy, in the name of Jesus."

Willy, fingers still jammed in his ears, stopped swearing. He stood in silence, stiff and unbending, his hostile eyes fixed on Mark.

"God loves you, Willy, and we're here to help you."

Willy didn't move.

"You need to take a bath now and get ready for bed."

He still refused to budge.

Mark grabbed him by the arm and smacked him on the bottom. "I've had enough of this behavior," he said firmly. "This is your last chance to bathe by yourself. Do you understand?"

Willy slowly started pulling off his clothes.

"When you're finished, come down to my office. We're going to have a little talk."

Mark went downstairs and Paul stood outside the bathroom door, waiting for Willy.

"Paul," Willy called, "do you think that man would let me go and live with him?"

"What? Willy, just take your bath."

When he was cleaned up and ready for bed, Willy bolted down the stairs to Mark's office.

"Well, you look a lot better," Mark said.

"Can I come live at your house?" Willy asked as he scrambled up on a chair.

"Come over here," Mark said.

Willy went over to him and Mark scooped him up on his lap.

"Willy, I'm going to pray for you right now and ask Jesus to come into your life. Is that okay?"

"Yeah, I guess so."

Mark prayed and when he finished, Willy was sitting there staring at him.

"Now can I come live with you?"

Mark laughed. "You're a persistent little rascal, aren't you? If you'll excuse me for a minute while I make a phone call, I'll let you know."

Willy jumped off Mark's lap and scurried out of the office. Mark shook his head and picked up the phone.

"Pam, I'd like to bring Willy to our house tonight, but only if you're comfortable with it."

"That's up to you, Mark. I trust your judgement. If you think it's okay, then it's okay with me."

"We'll be there in a few minutes."

On the way over, Willy said to Mark, "I can't wait to meet your wife."

"Why?"

"Because of what I'm going to do to her."

Mark wondered what was going on in that little mind. For a minute, he wondered if he should be taking him home.

Pam greeted them at the door and Willy gave her a big hug and a kiss. A French kiss.

"Willy!" Pam said, pulling away from him. "You don't kiss a lady like that. You can kiss me on the cheek."

Willy smirked.

Pam looked at Mark and said, "Well, this should be interesting."

As the weeks went by, Willy got more and more attached to Mark and Pam. One day he overheard them discussing whether to have a baby right away. Mark was looking forward to having children of his own again.

Willy marched into the room and said to Pam, "If you get pregnant, I'll get a knife and cut your stomach open and rip the baby out. I'm your kid and you don't need to have another one." Then he stomped off to his room.

"I don't believe this kid," Pam said, shocked.

"Does he frighten you?" Mark asked.

Pam hesitated. "No, not really. But he's become too possessive. I need to have a talk with him about it."

"I'm not surprised that he behaves the way he does. Look what he's been exposed to already: pornography, drinking, abuse, running in the streets; all before he was eight years old. The judge told his mother that if he didn't get help now, Willy had the capability of wiping out fifty people by the time he became an adult. And he'd do it without batting an eyelash."

"But I've also seen that other side of him, the sensitive side," Pam said. "Last night I walked into his room to say good night and he was singing songs to the Lord. Of course, he stopped as soon as he realized I was listening. I see the beginning of some changes in him. The hard part is knowing he has to leave eventually and possibly go back to that same environment." She closed her eyes and leaned back in her chair.

"All we can do is plant some positive seeds in his life," Mark said. "Let's pray that when he gets older, he'll look back and remember that someone really loved him and that it will make a difference."

She looked at Mark and smiled. "It's already made a difference in so many of them. And there will be a lot more."

"I hope so."

"Why do you 'hope so'? What's the matter?"

"We had another fire inspection."

"But we got the fire escape installed."

"Now it's the wiring. They said it's an old building and they feel the wiring isn't safe. They're concerned about a fire breaking out."

"But we've put so much into the building already. When is it all going to stop?"

"It's stopping right now."

"What do you mean?"

"It simply isn't worth dumping more money into an old building that doesn't even have the capacity that we need."

"What are you going to do?"

"What we need to do is start looking for another place, or some land to build on. With only $45 in the checking account as of today, it should be interesting. But we're facing another threat of being shut down if we don't comply."

Pam got up out of her chair and started pacing back and forth.

"How can they do that to us? Don't they realize what we're doing out here?" Her voice rose an octave. "We've already had hundreds of boys pass through our doors. Where would they be if we hadn't been able to help them and provide a place for them to stay? Some of the boys come from homes that never had electrical wiring, for goodness sake. What's wrong with these people anyway?" Anger lit up her eyes.

"We don't have any choice, Pam. I'm as frustrated as you. But we have no choice. We need to ask God to open up some new doors for us. I'm discouraged, but I'm not giving up." He spoke with determination, but his underlying concern came through.

Chapter Nineteen

"Mark!" Pam shouted out the car window, as she pulled into the driveway in front of Anchor House.

Mark was outside with a few of the boys and he walked over to the car, opening the door for her.

"I've got great news!" she said, throwing her arms around him. "I just got back from the doctor and I'm pregnant."

"For sure?"

"For sure. I knew you'd be happy about it."

"I am," he said. Then he called over to the boys. "Hey guys, guess what? We're going to have a baby!"

"Hey, Pop, that's great!" they shouted back.

"We'll be cramped with a baby in the trailer," Pam said, "but we'll manage."

"Maybe not so cramped."

Pam looked at him.

"I have some news, too." He grinned, waiting for her to ask what it was.

"Well? Come on, don't keep me in suspense."

"Witta Reynolds talked to me about the Upper Room where we've been meeting for prayer. She feels that God has been telling her to do something more with the house."

"That's a beautiful old home," Pam said. "But it's really not big enough for Anchor House, is it?

"No, that's not what she had in mind. She's giving *us* the house."

"You mean she'd let us rent it? Mark, we don't even have enough money for rent."

"She's giving us the deed to the house. It's ours. To live in. Just us."

"Praise God." Pam's eyes filled with tears.

The house had been a nightclub at one time, then was converted to a home. The living room was very large with an artificial brick fireplace. Plenty of room for having prayer meetings. The three bedrooms and two baths would be a luxury compared to how they had lived for the past several years.

"What about Anchor House?" Pam looked up at the house, then around the property. A few of the boys were playing basketball. Don Butcher was mowing the lawn. "We can't lose this," she said.

"I don't know what we're going to do. I'm trying to take it a day at a time. Most of the time I love this ministry, but when I have to deal with these financial crises, I hate it. I ask myself if it's all worth it. Maybe I should just go to work full-time and we can just take a kid at a time into our own home."

A horn blasted at the end of the driveway and Mark and Pam looked in that direction. A large trailer truck slowly made its way over to them.

"I wonder who that is," Mark said. "I'm not expecting any deliveries that I know of."

The truck stopped and a black driver stepped out. He walked over to Mark with a broad smile on his face.

"Remember me?"

Mark studied his face for a minute.

"Hey, Pop. It's me. Charles."

"Charles!" Mark threw his arms around him. "You look great!"

"I'm doing great. You see that truck? It's mine." He pulled some pictures out of his wallet. "I'm married now and have two kids."

Mark and Pam looked at the pictures and the three of them chatted back and forth for a few minutes.

"I didn't come out here just to show you pictures," he said, getting serious. "I came out to thank you for what you did for me when I was living here at Anchor House. It turned my life around. My wife and I are Christians and we're active in our church. I just want you to know that your labor isn't in vain. I know how rough you have it sometimes and you must get discouraged. Well, just look at me, " He walked around in a circle with his arms raised. "...a living, breathing miracle."

Joy lit up Mark's face. "Thanks for coming by," he said. "I needed this today."

Charles hopped back in his truck and backed out of the driveway, pulling on his air horn as he left.

"Hey, Pop!" One of the boys came running out of the house waving a newspaper in his hand. "Your picture's in the paper." He held it up for Mark and Pam to see.

"Mark Rivera honored for 'Service To Mankind'," he read proudly. "How about that, Pop? You won an award. I'm going to show the others." He dashed back into the house.

"God's perfect timing." Pam said. "He knows when we need to be encouraged."

Pam left and Mark went into his office. He reached for his Bible and began reading in Matthew 25: "I was hungry, and you gave Me something to eat; I was thirsty, and you gave Me drink; I was a stranger, and you invited Me in; naked, and you clothed Me; I was sick, and you visited Me; I was in prison, and you came to Me. "

He put down the Bible and picked up the phone. He dialed the number of one of his board members.

"We need to start a building fund right away," Mark said.

The people in Auburndale and surrounding areas responded to the needs of Anchor House and the funds for building a new facility began flowing in. Churches, businesses, a bank, Girl Scouts, Lions Club, V.F.W., Rotary Club and others donated various amounts. Agrico Mining

Company donated ten acres of land. The mother of one of Anchor House board members gave a single gift of $50,000. Another board member, Gordonn Dirkes, designed the buildings. Articles continued to appear in the local newspapers, spreading the Anchor House message.

In 1984, the new facility opened, having passed all inspections. It included a residence for house parents, an office area, five bedrooms, a living-dining area, kitchen, a storage area, a walk-in freezer, and a game room.

Over a period of time there were several changes in staff, with people leaving and moving on to other things. Luciano Rivera (no relation to Mark) joined the staff as Administrator. He had many years of experience working with juvenile services. Joe Akins, a student at Southeastern Bible College, worked at Anchor House on weekends and his parents eventually moved down from Georgia to be the live-in house parents for the boys. The boys loved Mrs. Akins' Italian cooking. A full-time secretary came on board and volunteers helped in various other capacities.

All of this allowed Pam to spend more of her time with her own children who were born during this time of raising funds and moving into the new facility. They had a son, Matthew, and a daughter, Theresa. Mark also began taking classes at the Institute for Christian Studies in Orlando, with his goal being ordination as a Deacon in the Episcopal Church. So it was a busy time.

But just when everything started to fall into place and some of the major hurdles overcome, another crisis hit.

"Anchor House Almost Closed," read the headlines in the *Auburndale Star*. Reporter, Sherri Nestico, told the story of Mark going to court and being granted an emergency restraining order to keep the home open. It was all about being late in filing an audit.

" 'I cannot believe how the HRS officials are treating this situation,' Rivera said. 'They are making decisions based on technicalities, without regard for the well-being of the boys in this home. What is more important than the children?

"You always hear complaints about the overcrowding in foster homes, and here you have a beautiful, big home that houses only 20 boys,' he said. 'These guys never go hungry, they have a roof over their heads, they get lots of love. It simply amazes me that HRS is so willing to close us down on such a small technicality.

"I have no problem with HRS wanting the audit. I'm just against them putting stress on the kids by threatening to close us down.' "

Attorney Adrian Gabaldon represented Anchor House and saw to it that the audit was turned in to HRS. They said it was unacceptable and threatened to close the doors again.

Gabaldon told a reporter, "There is a one-line statement on the cover letter a CPA writes for audits. It says that the CPA certifies the audit to be complete. On the audit Anchor House turned in, the statement said that the report was a compilation... That's what HRS is concerned with.

"For years, Anchor House has been turning in compilations and they have been accepted. Now, the district office requirements have changed. All along, we thought the compilations were okay. HRS would never say exactly what they wanted, just that they wanted an audit. Well, an audit means a lot of different things. We could never get them to pinpoint what they were looking for.

"The accountant has estimated that to make a full audit of the time frame they want would cost between $10,000 and $20,000."

People familiar with Mark and the Anchor House began to respond. State Representative Fred Jones wrote to the HRS secretary on behalf of Anchor House. Mr. Jones told a reporter, "They may not always hear the voice of the public, but they do hear the voice of people who approve their budget. It burns me up. With all its silly rules, HRS doesn't have any room to talk about 'procedures'. Those folks over there are tangled up in their own underwear. In this bureaucratic maze of technical positions, my frustration level occasionally boils over, and this is a prime example. But, we shall overcome and Anchor House will stay open."

That was just the beginning of hundreds of letters that poured in.

From United States Senator Paula Hawkins to the secretary of HRS: "I am writing in behalf of Anchor House Ministries of Polk County, Florida. As you know, Anchor House has been serving abused and neglected children in Florida for over twelve years...I am personally familiar with their fine work and am very impressed with the feeling of home and family that they provide these children..."

From United States Senator Lawton Chiles, in response to a call for help from an Anchor House supporter: "While I have no authority over decisions made by HRS...I have contacted the officials on your behalf in an effort to ensure your views receive proper consideration."

From Circuit Judge Randall McDonald: "We need Anchor House here in Polk County, and we need it to continue to be what it has been; something for children to hold fast to..."

From Bishop William Folwell of the Episcopal Diocese of Central Florida: "Certainly the presence of Christ is manifested at Anchor House..."

The *Auburndale Star* ran an article titled "HRS May Close Anchor House," by Bill Fusselle. It showed the Auburndale Lions Club presenting a check to Anchor House to help with the cost of the audit. The article quoted Mark as saying, 'I only have four HRS kids in here right now, and I don't even get enough from the state to support them. Of the $580 per month HRS gives Anchor House for each HRS-sponsored boy, part of that money goes to the individual.

'I don't have any foundations. I have to depend on the community. I get very discouraged at times. I figure, what's the use? That's how I'm feeling right now.

'If they decide to close us down, I'd like to know where my 20 boys are going to go all of a sudden. It's causing them real emotional problems right now. They don't understand it.

I feel like HRS is coming to my house taking my kids away, and I don't know how to fight them.' "

Mary Toothman said in her article in the *Polk Tribune*: "Are you listening, Tallahassee? Florida's taxpayers are talking to you folks up there in the main offices of the Department of Health and Rehabilitative Services. They're telling you not to close down Anchor House, a home for unwanted boys. They're saying that children's lives are sometimes more important than rules.

"More than 500 names have been put on various petitions ... Telephones in politicians' offices have been ringing...One person even wrote to President Ronald Reagan... People are sending in money to help cover the cost of the audit...Mark Rivera is encouraged...Are you listening, Tallahassee?"

Mark sat at his desk reading a letter from a friend: "I want you to know that I really am sharing your concern for your boys at Anchor House. You are in my prayers. God will see you through all of this and you will be all the stronger for it. Let me share a couple of my favorite Scriptures that have ministered to me during trying circumstances.

'Count it all joy, my brethren, when you meet various trials, for you know that the testing of your faith produces steadfastness. And let steadfastness have its full effect, that you may be perfect and complete, lacking in nothing.' (James 1:2-4)

'So take a new grip with your tired hands, stand firm on your shaky legs, and mark out a straight, smooth path for your feet so that those who follow you, though weak and lame, will not fall and hurt themselves, but become strong.' (Hebrews 12:12-13)

"Mark, in the midst of this 'mess' you've got lots of people, especially your boys watching to see how you handle things. As they watch you, they will be learning valuable lessons. Most came from families where their parents responded to crisis in a much different way. It is so hard not to be hurt, angry and resentful when the whole world seems to be out to get you, but God will see you through this and you and your boys and all who are touched by your life, will be blessed by it.

We love you, Mark, and appreciate your courage and strength to stand firm."

Mark leaned back in his chair and whispered, "Thank you, God!"

Chapter Twenty

The HRS crisis passed, with Anchor House receiving full approval and licensed as a group home. On Monday, March 2, 1987, Mark Rivera's ordination service was held at St. Alban's Episcopal Church in Auburndale, Florida.

Everyone stood as the overcrowded church reverberated with the sound of joyous music as the Bishop, clergy and choir came in procession down to the altar.

Bishop Folwell's voice echoed, "Blessed be God: Father, Son and Holy Spirit."

The people responded: "And blessed be His kingdom, now and for ever. Amen."

Everyone was seated while the Presenters stood before the Bishop: "William, Bishop in the Church of God, on behalf of the clergy and people of the Diocese of Central Florida, we present to you Mark Rivera to be ordained a deacon in Christ's holy catholic Church."

After the presentation, Bishop Folwell motioned for the audience to rise again as he said, "Dear friends in Christ, you know the importance of this ministry, and the weight of your responsibility in presenting Mark for ordination to the sacred order of deacons. Therefore, if any of you know any impediment or crime because of which we should not proceed, come forward now and make it known."

During that moment of silence, Mark thought of his past life...that young, frightened boy arriving in New York City, the years of drugs and violence, serving time in prison... Tears of gratitude towards God splashed down his cheeks as Mark thought of God's forgiveness, love and faithfulness.

Seated again, the audience recited the Nicene Creed. Then Mark stood alone before Bishop Folwell.

"My brother, every Christian is called to follow Jesus Christ, serving God the Father, through the power of the Holy Spirit. God now calls you to a special ministry of servanthood directly under your Bishop. In the name of Jesus Christ, you are to serve all people, particularly the poor, the weak, the sick, and the lonely."

"My brother, do you believe that you are truly called by God and His Church to the life and work of a deacon?"

"I believe I am so called," Mark answered.

"May the Lord by His Grace uphold you in the service He lays upon you."

"Amen."

Mark knelt as the Bishop stood and laid hands on him while reciting the Prayer of Consecration.

"Let His life and teaching so reflect your commandments, that through Him many may come to know you and love you. As your Son came not to be served but to serve, may this deacon share in Christ's service, and come to the unending glory of Him who, with you and the Holy Spirit, lives and reigns, one God, for ever and ever."

And the people said, "Amen!"

The stole vestment was ceremoniously placed across Mark's white robe. The Bishop then handed Mark a Bible as he said with his full, rich voice, "Receive this Bible as the sign of your authority to proclaim God's Word and to assist in the ministration of His Holy Sacraments."

Communion was prepared and the congregation was invited forward to receive. Pam stepped forward and knelt, holding out her hands to receive communion from her husband.

At the close of the service, Mark's voice resounded throughout the church, "Let us go forth into the world, rejoicing in the power of the Spirit."

The people responded vibrantly, "Thanks be to God!"

Epilogue
Mark Rivera

As I look back on my life, I see that God has brought me from addiction and a life on the streets of New York City to my ordination as a deacon in the Episcopal Church. I have watched the boys pass through Anchor House and I sometimes ask, "God, why did you choose me for this work? I feel so inadequate." Yet, my heart goes out to these broken children. I've had a burden for hurting boys ever since God touched my own life. Now my dream is to see each one of these boys touched by the Father's hand.

I think of the Jewish boy, Robin, who came to us. I did not attack his religion and try to convince him that Jesus was the Messiah. I simply showed him love. Through that love he was drawn to Jesus and is now studying for the ministry. He has a Christian wife and three beautiful children.

Another boy, Charles, came to us from Michigan. He was kicked out of his house by his step-father at age 16 and assigned to us by HRS. He was angry, rebellious, and didn't want to be at Anchor House. But we showed him love. Eventually, Charles believed it was real and began to respond. He began to see that all his so-called friends could care less if he was starving in the streets. But here at Anchor House, people genuinely cared.

Now his social worker calls him her only real success story. He recently graduated from high school. Had he stayed in the 'system' he would have been bounced from one foster home to another and probably ended up in serious trouble. Now he talks about showing other kids that somebody cares about them.

I am reminded of a TV commercial that used the slogan, 'Pay me now, or pay me later.' That's so true of these boys. If we reach them in time, they won't end up on the streets as addicts, or find themselves in prison. There are many programs that work with those who have already wrecked their lives. My vision for Anchor House is to reach the boys before they get thrown into the turbulent waters; to rescue them before they get into serious trouble.

Jesus said, "Suffer little children, and forbid them not, to come unto me: for of such is the kingdom of heaven." (Matthew 19:14) Christ cared and He is our example. Anchor House is Jesus' love in action. It's fine to reach overseas to the starving children and include them in our mission giving, but let's not forget those right here in our own backyard. There are thousands of starving boys: starving for food, for a home, for someone who cares. Jesus said, "First go to Jerusalem, and in all Judaea, and in Samaria, and unto the uttermost part of the earth." (Acts 1:8) We need to start right in Jerusalem, in our own community.

I'm not looking for a world-wide ministry. I'm simply looking to follow Jesus' example and work with a few. Then, those few will multiply into thousands. I want to duplicate myself in Anchor House. I want these boys to leave here with a burden for others like themselves. I want them to pass on the same unconditional love that they have received.

My vision for the future of Anchor House is to find a sponsor for every boy who comes to us, someone who will make one boy a part of their family. Those who have done this have found that in giving of themselves they have been blessed with richer lives.

One of the things I have learned over the years is that all God requires of you and me is for us to be willing to put love into action. He'll provide the rest. He has proven that over and over again through the ministry here at Anchor House.

At Anchor House we truly have been blessed by the touch of the Father's hand.

Vision For The Future of Anchor House

Sometime ago I dreamed I was in a place where I could see children of all ages crying out in loud voices saying, "Please help us! Please love us! We are hurting! Please hear us." I saw Jesus Christ point to me as he said, "Mark, help those children of mine. Be a father to them. Help them know that there is love in this earthly world. I will supply you with all you need to help them." Christ took me by the hand and showed me a community with many different buildings... a building for recreation, one for learning different vocations; and even a chapel built from logs. When I awakened I was covered with sweat. My dream had been so awesomely real.

I dream of facilities and manpower to expand what we have accomplished so far. Our work has only just begun. I can't lay out detailed plans for Anchor House in this book, but I can say that our needs are constantly changing and in order to grow and meet the needs of the boys in our community I envision new buildings and expanded services and programs.

I see lives being changed, I see hurt and pain melting away, and I see boys being touched by this ministry whose lives will never again be the same. That touch is truly the touch of the Father's hand. Through this ministry lives are touched every day and and I thank the Lord for the kind and generous support that has allowed this ministry to continue. I pray that our new vision will soon come to pass. I hope that you can be a part of this vision. The Father touches all those who answer the call to do His work.

I have a dream. I ask your prayers and support in making this dream a reality. Jesus said, "Suffer not the little children to come unto me because of such is the the kingdom of Heaven." Our future rests in the hands of our children. Your support will enable me to help them. Without you, our loving supporters and friends, and without the Lord's, help Anchor House could not exist. Thank you.

In His Love,

Mark "Pop" Rivera